PEOPLE
AROUND
THE WORLD

Edited and designed by Toucan Books Limited, London
Editorial consultant Keith Lye

For Kingfisher Publications Plc
Managing editor Melissa Fairley
Editorial Sheila Clewley
Coordinating editor Stephanie Pliakas
Art director Mike Davis
DTP coordinator Sarah Pfitzner
DTP operator Primrose Burton
Production controller Debbie Otter
Picture research Rachael Swann

KINGFISHER
a Houghton Mifflin Company imprint
215 Park Avenue South
New York, New York 10003
www.houghtonmifflinbooks.com

First published in 2002
10 9 8 7 6 5 4 3 2 1

1TR/TWP/CLSN(CLSN)/130MA

Copyright © Kingfisher Publications Plc 2002

LIBRARY OF CONGRESS CATALOGING-IN-PUBLICATION DATA
has been applied for.

ISBN 0-7534-5497-1

Color separations by Colourscan
Printed in Singapore

Collecting water

*For many people getting clean water involves more than
turning on a faucet. These schoolchildren in Zimbabwe in
Africa are lining up at the village water pump.*

PEOPLE AROUND THE WORLD

Antony Mason

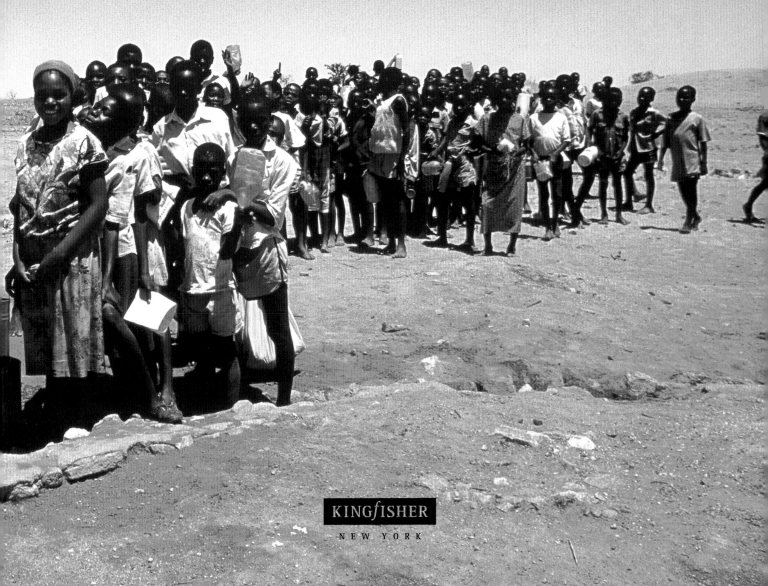

KINGFISHER

NEW YORK

Contents

Net gains

*A fisherman in Lake Inle in Myanmar
(Burma) drops cylindrically shaped
nets to the bottom of the lake and
then spears the fish caught in the nets.*

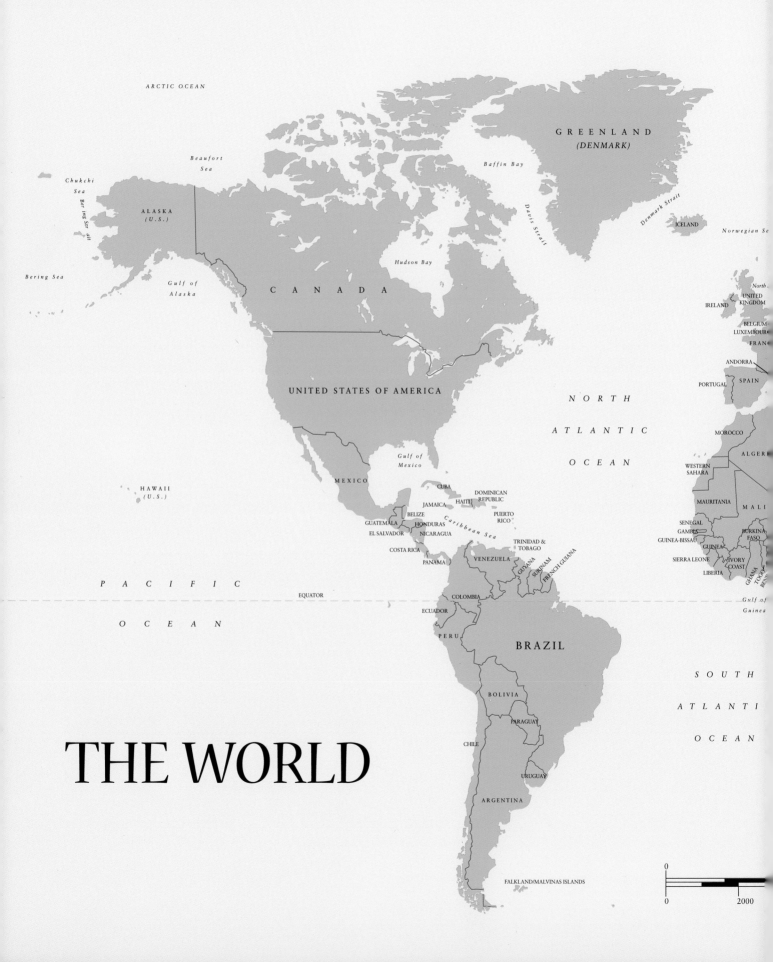

ARCTIC OCEAN

Beaufort Sea

Chukchi Sea

GREENLAND
(DENMARK)

Baffin Bay

Bering Strait

ALASKA
(U.S.)

Davis Strait

Denmark Strait

ICELAND

Norwegian Se

Bering Sea

Gulf of Alaska

C A N A D A

Hudson Bay

North

IRELAND

UNITED KINGDOM

BELGIUM
LUXEMBOUR•
FRAN•

UNITED STATES OF AMERICA

N O R T H

ANDORRA

PORTUGAL

SPAIN

A T L A N T I C

MOROCCO

O C E A N

ALGER•

HAWAII
(U.S.)

Gulf of Mexico

WESTERN
SAHARA

MEXICO

CUBA

DOMINICAN
REPUBLIC

MAURITANIA

MALI

JAMAICA

HAITI

PUERTO
RICO

SENEGAL

BELIZE

Caribbean Sea

GAMBIA

BURKINA
FASO

GUATEMALA

HONDURAS

GUINEA-BISSAU

GUINEA

EL SALVADOR

NICARAGUA

SIERRA LEONE

IVORY
COAST

COSTA RICA

TRINIDAD &
TOBAGO

LIBERIA

GHANA
TOGO
BENI•

PANAMA

VENEZUELA

GUYANA

SURINAM

FRENCH GUIANA

P A C I F I C

EQUATOR

COLOMBIA

Gulf of Guinea

ECUADOR

O C E A N

PERU

BRAZIL

S O U T H

BOLIVIA

A T L A N T I

PARAGUAY

O C E A N

THE WORLD

CHILE

URUGUAY

ARGENTINA

FALKLAND/MALVINAS ISLANDS

0

0   2000

ARCTIC OCEAN

ARCTIC OCEAN

Laptev Sea

Kara Sea

East Siberian Sea

Barents Sea

Chukchi Sea

Bering Strait

ORWAY

SWEDEN FINLAND

R U S S I A

Sea of Okhotsk

Bering Sea

ESTONIA

NMARK LATVIA

Baltic Sea LITHUANIA

ETHERLANDS RUSSIA

ERMANY BELARUS

POLAND

CZECH SLOVAK
EICH REP. REP.

ZITZERLAND HUNGARY UKRAINE

SLOVENIA MOLDOVA

CROATIA ROMANIA

OSNIA UNION OF
ERZEGOVINA SERBIA AND BULGARIA
MONTENEGRO

ITALY MACEDONIA GEORGIA

ALBANIA ARMENIA

GREECE TURKEY AZERBAIJAN

KAZAKHSTAN

Aral Sea

UZBEKISTAN KYRGYZSTAN

TURKMENISTAN

TAJIKISTAN

MONGOLIA

C H I N A

NORTH
KOREA *Sea of Japan*

SOUTH
KOREA JAPAN

Caspian Sea

Black Sea

Mediterranean Sea

TUNISIA

CYPRUS
LEBANON SYRIA

ISRAEL

IRAQ IRAN

JORDAN KUWAIT

LIBYA

EGYPT *Red Sea*

SAUDI
ARABIA

BAHRAIN
QATAR

UNITED
ARAB
EMIRATES

OMAN

AFGHANISTAN

PAKISTAN

NEPAL BHUTAN

*Yellow
Sea*

*East
China Sea*

TAIWAN

P A C I F I C

O C E A N

GER

CHAD

ERITREA

YEMEN

Gulf of Aden

DJIBOUTI

GERIA

SUDAN

I N D I A

BANGLADESH

MYANMAR LAOS

THAILAND VIETNAM

CAMBODIA

*South
China
Sea*

PHILIPPINES

Philippine Sea

*Bay of
Bengal*

CENTRAL
AFRICAN
REPUBLIC

AMEROON

ETHIOPIA

SOMALIA

SRI
LANKA

BRUNEI

MALAYSIA *Celebes
Sea*

EQUATORIAL
GUINEA

UGANDA KENYA

GABON

CONGO

DEMOCRATIC
REPUBLIC OF
CONGO

RWANDA
BURUNDI

TANZANIA

I N D O N E S I A

PAPUA
NEW
GUINEA

SOLOMON
ISLANDS

I N D I A N

O C E A N

ANGOLA

ZAMBIA MALAWI

MOZAMBIQUE

MADAGASCAR

MAURITIUS

Mozambique Channel

RÉUNION

Coral Sea

VANUATU

FIJI

NAMIBIA ZIMBABWE

BOTSWANA

NEW CALEDONIA

SWAZILAND

A U S T R A L I A

LESOTHO

SOUTH
AFRICA

N

Tasman Sea NEW
ZEALAND

00	4000	6000	8000 Miles (at equator)

4000	6000	8000	10 000	12 000 Kilometres (at equator)

INTRODUCTION

When astronauts look down upon Earth from space, they often remark on how beautiful it appears—a spinning jewel of blue and green and wispy clouds surrounded by endless, velvety darkness.

More remarkable, however, is the dazzling variety of people within each continent. In small clearings in the Amazonian rain forest of Brazil there are people who follow a way of life that has barely changed for thousands of years, while the Brazilian city streets of São Paulo throb with traffic and shoppers in pursuit of the latest fashions.

In Bangalore in India some of the world's leading computer experts tap away at their keyboards in air-conditioned offices, while in monasteries in valleys high in the Himalayas, Buddhist monks use ancient knowledge and chants in their search for eternal peace.

In Canada farmers harvest huge fields of ripe wheat with fleets of combines, while lone Inuit hunters set out across the ice with their rifles and harpoons to catch seals.

From space, astronauts can see all of the geographical features of each continent— the coastlines, the plains, the mountains and valleys, the deserts, and the ice caps surrounding the poles. Geography helps to explain why people in certain parts of the world lead such different lives. Landscape and climate determine what grows in each region, what people can eat, and how they can survive.

Cultural beginnings

Human beings like us have existed for about 100,000 years. Civilization and the complex world of cities, trade, government, military power, organized religion, writing, and art have existed for about 7,000 years. Over long periods of time people have developed their own clear ideas about how best to live in their lands—not just what to grow and eat but also what clothes to wear, what type of houses to build, what languages to speak, what gods to worship, what musical instruments to play, and what games to enjoy. In other words, they have evolved their own cultures.

Isolated communities with little or no contact with the rest of the world develop very distinct patterns of life. For example, in Papua New Guinea there are numerous remote villages in the mountains—so remote that many have developed their own languages, which even people living in the next valley cannot understand. As a result Papua New Guinea has more than 700 languages.

Global influence

Most communities have had contact with the outside world for thousands of years

Mountain land

The small country of Nepal lies in the Himalaya mountains and is home to the world's highest peak—Mount Everest.

through trade, travel, conquest, and migration. This contact with other peoples has a very strong influence on how we lead our lives.

Potatoes, tomatoes, and chocolate, for example, were unknown to the world outside the Americas before the arrival of European explorers in the 1500s. Now through the process of trade they are found all around the world. Ideas and religions also travel around the world. Indian traders arriving by sea brought Islam to Southeast Asia in the 1200s.

The global influence of cultures has speeded up in recent years through developments in transportation and communications. Now mangoes and other tropical fruits can be flown across the world—one day they are

on a tree in a Caribbean island, and a few days later they are on the shelves of supermarkets in Europe. Through satellite communications we can talk to—even see— someone on the other side of the world.

The effect of sharing ideas and products through trade and communications is that cultures around the world are becoming increasingly similar. Some people are concerned by this and feel that many unique cultures are under threat. But in many cases this process, known as globalization, looks like progress. The lives of many millions of people have been made considerably better through modern medicine, which was largely developed in the Western world. But the impact of exploration and industrial development in remote regions has also exposed native populations to new diseases against which they have no natural resistence, and the adoption of new ways of life can be at the expense of local traditions.

Festive fun

At the annual Ati-Atihan Festival in the Philippines children dress up in colorful costumes to enjoy the noisy street parties.

International culture

Today in many parts of the world everyday culture has an international influence. Modern pop music is a blend of cultures from around the world with roots in Europe, the U.S., the Caribbean, South America, Africa, the Middle East, and India. Our supermarkets and restaurants are full of foods from an even greater range of countries. We may want this variety of food, but it means that our local diets will change and possibly vanish forever.

There are other social and political implications of this process of globalization. For example, in most countries of the world child labor is against the law, and there are welfare systems to protect the poor. But some of the goods, fruits, and vegetables imported from other countries may have been made or picked by workers—sometimes children—who earn very low wages. However, some people argue that low pay is better than no pay—many workers would not survive without these meager wages.

Meanwhile the population of the world is growing fast. Currently it stands at more than

School lunches

Japanese schoolchildren use chopsticks to eat their meals.

six billion and is likely to rise by half as much again, to nine billion, by 2050. China's population is 1.2 billion—the same as the population of the entire world just one hundred years ago. This rapid rise in population—largely owing to improvements in medicine and better standards of health—is putting increasing pressure on the land and resources.

Sense of identity

When people and nations feel themselves under pressure and threat—be it from lack of food or water or from aggression by other nations—they tend to reinforce their sense of identity. They like to define what it is that

Cultural mix

This youth group has been sponsored by the New York Police Department (NYPD). Many similar inner-city schemes are being developed to improve race relations.

makes them feel different from other peoples or nations. It could be their language, their religion, their land, or even the type of food they eat. This identity gives them a sense of place in their world, reflecting their history and origins.

When disputes arise with other nations or groups, people sometimes rally around their identity—represented by flags, symbols, and national anthems—and this nationalism can be the cause of war. Like globalization, a strong sense of cultural and national identity has both advantages and disadvantages.

Struggles and war are an unfortunate by-product of cultural and religious differences—the same differences that supply the immense richness and variety of human life on earth. And all too often conflict can obscure extraordinary achievements found in all parts of the world.

ARCTIC AND SUBARCTIC

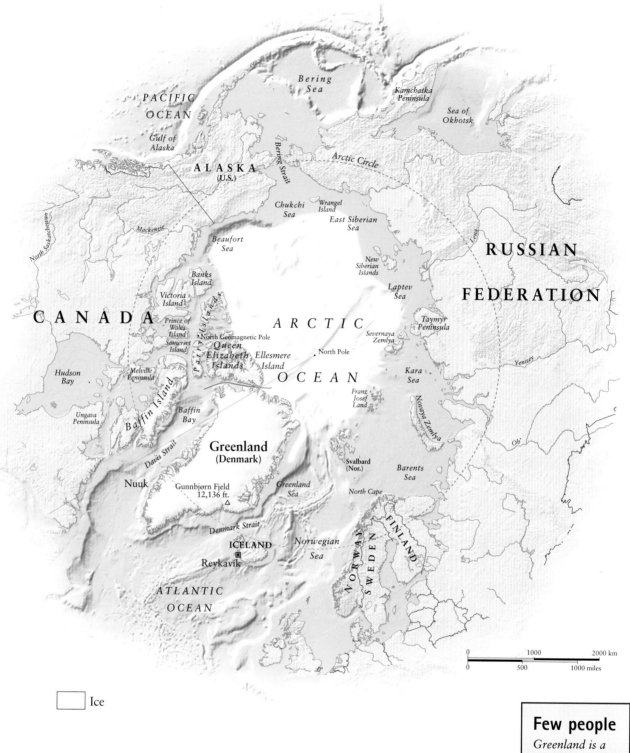

PACIFIC
OCEAN

*Bering
Sea*

*Kamchatka
Peninsula*

*Sea of
Okhotsk*

*Gulf of
Alaska*

ALASKA
(U.S.)

Arctic Circle

*Bering
Strait*

*Chukchi
Sea*

*Wrangel
Island*

*East Siberian
Sea*

RUSSIAN

North Saskatchewan

Mackenzie

*Beaufort
Sea*

*New
Siberian
Islands*

Lena

FEDERATION

*Banks
Island*

*Laptev
Sea*

CANADA

*Victoria
Island*

ARCTIC

*Taymyr
Peninsula*

Yenisey

*Prince of
Wales
Island*

Parry Islands

North Geomagnetic Pole

*Severnaya
Zemlya*

*Somerset
Island*

*Queen
Elizabeth
Islands*

*Ellesmere
Island*

· North Pole

OCEAN

*Kara
Sea*

*Hudson
Bay*

*Melville
Peninsula*

Baffin Island

*Franz
Josef
Land*

Novaya Zemlya

Ob'

*Ungava
Peninsula*

*Baffin
Bay*

Greenland
(Denmark)

*Svalbard
(Nor.)*

*Barents
Sea*

Davis Strait

Nuuk

*Gunnbjørn Fjeld
12,136 ft.*
△

*Greenland
Sea*

North Cape

Denmark Strait

*Norwegian
Sea*

NORWAY

SWEDEN

FINLAND

ICELAND ◉

Reykavík

ATLANTIC

OCEAN

0°

| 0 | 1000 | 2000 km |
| 0 | 500 | 1000 miles |

☐ Ice

Northern land

*Canada, Greenland,
Finland, Iceland,
Norway, Russia, Sweden,
and Alaska have land
within the Arctic Circle.*

Few people

*Greenland is a
self-governing
province of
Denmark. It is
50 times larger
than Denmark
but only has the
population of
a small town.*

THE ARCTIC AND SUBARCTIC

The far north of the world is covered by the Arctic Ocean, with a sea so cold that much of the surface is coated in ice. As the winter approaches the ice spreads out from the polar ice cap and joins up with land, covering the top of the world in a thick, white blanket. Despite winter temperatures of −40°F (−40°C) people have lived in these regions for many years.

Inuit life

The Inuit (previously known as Eskimo) people inhabit Greenland, the northern coasts and islands of Canada, northern Alaska, and the north coast of Russia, where they are known as Yupik.

In the past the Inuit lived by hunting and fishing. They traveled in kayaks (canoes) and on sleds drawn by husky dogs, looking for seals, fish, and arctic hares. They dried the meat and fish to preserve it. This gave them food for the winter when they returned to their villages.

The Inuit make warm clothes and boots from animal furs and fishhooks and harpoons from bones. They have a very strong sense of community and traditionally rub noses as a greeting.

Keeping warm

Inuit children wear sealskin and caribou jackets to protect them from the harsh Arctic conditions.

Ice fishing

Inuit fishermen make small holes in the ice- and snow-covered lakes and let down fishing nets or rods into the water.

The Inuit are famous for their round ice houses called igloos. These are surprisingly snug inside, but igloos were mostly used as temporary shelters for hunters on the ice, and this is still their main use today. In their villages the Inuit lived in small cabins made of boulders, turf, whalebone, and driftwood.

New ways

The lives of the Inuit have changed over the last 50 years. Today most of them live in houses premade in factories and shipped in by boat or in modern apartment blocks in the larger towns. They ride snowmobiles instead of husky sleds and eat canned and packet food flown in from towns farther south. Some have jobs working in oil fields or in tourism.

Major efforts are being made to preserve Inuit traditions and their language. Inuktitut is spoken right across the region. In Canada the Inuit have been given their own land called Nunavut ("our land" in Inuktitut)— a vast territory of more than 780,000 sq. mi. (two million sq km) in the northeast.

GREENLAND

Status
Self-governing province
of Denmark
Capital
Godthaab
Area
840,000 sq. mi.
Population
56,309
Population density
15 per sq. mi.
Life expectancy
63 (m); 72 (f)
Religion
Christianity
Languages
Inuit, Greenlandic, Danish
Adult literacy rate
100 percent
Currency
Danish krone

Northern life

*Most people in Greenland live in
towns on the coast, but there is a
number of smaller settlements where
people live by hunting and fishing.*

EUROPE

ATLANTIC
OCEAN

Reykjavik ◾
ICELAND

Norwegian
Sea

North Cape

Vesterålen

Lofoten

NORWAY

SWEDEN

FINLAND

Kola
Peninsula

Faroe Is.

Shetland Is.

Orkney Is.

Outer Hebrides

Oslo ◾

Vänern

Stockholm ◾

Vättern

Gulf of Bothnia

Helsinki ◾

Gulf of Finland

Tallinn ◾
ESTONIA

Lake
Ladog

Saaremaa

Gotland

RIGA ◾
LATVIA

Öland

LITHUANIA

Vilnius ◾

Baltic
Sea

Bornholm

Russ. Fed.

◾ Minsk

BELARUS

REP. OF
IRELAND
Dublin ◾

UNITED
KINGDOM

North
Sea

DENMARK
COPENHAGEN ◾

Celtic
Sea

London ◾

NETHERLANDS
Amsterdam ◾

Berlin ◾

GERMANY

Elbe

Oder

◾ Warsaw

POLAND

◾ Kiev

UKRAINE

English Channel

Channel Is.

BELGIUM
Brussels ◾

LUXEMBOURG

Prague ◾

CZECH
REPUBLIC

Vistula

Carpathians

Dnister

Paris ◾

Luxembourg ◾

Bay of
Biscay

Seine

Loire

FRANCE

Rhine

SLOVAKIA

Vienna ◾ ◾ Bratislava

MOLDOV

Chisinău ◾

Berne ◾

Vaduz ◾
LIECH.

AUSTRIA

◾ Budapest

Mont Blanc △
15,770 ft.

SWITZ.
ALPS

Massif
Central

Garonne

Rhône

Po

SLOVENIA

Ljubljana ◾

HUNGARY

Tisza

ROMANIA

Andorra
La Vella

ANDORRA

Pyrenees

PORTUGAL

Duero

MONACO

Ligurian
Sea

SAN
MARINO

Zagreb ◾

CROATIA

BOSNIA-
HERZEGOVINA

◾ Belgrade

Bucharest ◾

Danube

Tagus

Lisbon ◾

◾ Madrid

SPAIN

Guadalquivir

Corsica

Appennines

Adriatic Sea

Sarajevo ◾

UNION OF
SERBIA AND
MONTENEGRO

BULGARIA

Sofia ◾

Rome ◾

VATICAN CITY

Majorca

Ibiza

Minorca

Balearic Islands

Sardinia

Tyrrhenian
Sea

Skopje ◾

Tirana ◾ MACEDONIA

ITALY

ALBANIA

GREECE

Aegean
Sea

Strait of Gibraltar

Sicily

△ Mt. Etna
10,955 ft.

Ionian
Sea

Athens ◾

Peloponnese

Rhodes

MALTA
◾ Valletta

Mediterranean
Sea

Crete

Mountain
Desert
Tundra
Cropland
Wetland
Needleleaf forest
Tropical rain forest
Temperate grassland
Ice

Novaya Zemlya

Barents
Sea

Pechora

Ural Mountains

NorthernDvina

ake
Onega

RUSSIAN

FEDERATION

Kama

Volga

Moscow

Ural

Volga

Don

Dnieper

Sea of
Azov

CRIMEA

Elbrus
△5642m

Caucasus

Caspian Sea

Black Sea

N

0   500   1000 km
0   250   500 miles

Smallest country

The smallest independent country in the world is Vatican City—literally a city inside another city (Rome).

Vast nation

Russia is the world's largest country. One fourth lies in Europe, and the other three fourths lie in Asia.

Troubled times

Eastern European states were once controlled by the Soviet Union and now face an uncertain economic future.

The Hexagon

France is the third largest country in Europe. The French call their country L'Hexagone (the hexagon) owing to its six-sided shape.

Euro zone

Fifteen countries are currently members of an economic alliance known since 1993 as the European Union. Twelve of these countries share a common currency—the euro.

SCANDINAVIA AND NORTHERN EUROPE

A great hook-shaped piece of land sticks out of Russia, curving around the Baltic Sea. It is divided into three countries—Finland, Sweden, and Norway. Across the narrow entrance to the Baltic Sea opposite Sweden lies Denmark, and about 620 mi. (1,000km) into the Atlantic Ocean lies the volcanic island of Iceland. These five countries are known as Scandinavia.

Fjord formation

Norway's famous fjords were formed during the last Ice Age. Glaciers cut through mountains, creating valleys that filled with water.

Fairy tale landmark

The Little Mermaid statue in Denmark's capital, Copenhagen, celebrates the work of Denmark's most famous writer, Hans Christian Andersen.

Land of the midnight sun

Each country in northwestern Europe has its own language, as well as its own culture and distinctive landscape—but they share a history. Their Viking ancestors were traders and seafarers. Originally from Norway, Sweden, and Denmark, the Vikings ventured from their homelands and settled across much of northern Europe from A.D. 700 to A.D. 1000. Norway became independent of Sweden only in 1905.

The Scandinavian countries have similar climates. Finland, Sweden, Norway, and the very northern tip of Iceland stretch into the Arctic Circle—which means long, dark, snowy winters. For some midsummer days in the Arctic region the sun does not set at all. This region is called the "land of the midnight sun."

There is good fishing in the North Atlantic and the Baltic, and many people in the cold north make a living from it. It is the main industry in Iceland. There are huge forests in Norway, Sweden, and Finland. In fact almost two thirds of Finland is covered by forests. The conifer trees are used to make timber, furniture, and paper.

The original settlers of the far north, the Lapps (or Sami, as they call themselves), still live by herding reindeer in the Arctic regions of Finland, Sweden, and Norway. Farther south, in the open countryside of Sweden, farmers grow wheat, oats, and potatoes. Denmark is famous for its bacon and dairy products. Norway is more mountainous. Huge mountains rise out of the sea along the west coast, creating fjords (steep-sided sea inlets). On the sheltered coasts of the fjords, warmed by the ocean current called the Gulf Stream, farmers can grow grain, vegetables, and fruits such as apples and pears.

Saunas and smorgasbords

Finland is famous for its saunas—rooms in which water is poured on hot coals so that the heat will make the bather's skin "sweat out" impurities. The southern part of the country is dotted with lakes, and the Finnish people build special cabins beside the lakes in which to use the saunas. After sitting in the heat for a while they run out and plunge into the lake's freezing water. In Iceland hot water is provided from the volcanic activity deep beneath the ground. This geothermal energy is tapped to provide heating for houses and greenhouses, and at the Svartseni geothermal power plant people can swim outdoors all year round in the human-made Blue Lagoon.

In the winter many people go skiing. There are ski resorts and ski lifts in the mountains of Norway, but cross-country skiing is also popular and especially suitable for the lowlands and lakes of Sweden and Finland. There is also tobogganing and skating.

Sailing, canoeing, fishing, and walking are popular summer pastimes. Summer is also the best time to enjoy a traditional Scandinavian meal, or smorgasbord. It is a buffet of dishes such as cold meats, shrimp, and smoked fish, as well as gravlax (slices of marinated salmon).

Lapp tradition

The Lapps (or Sami) live in northern Norway, Sweden, and Finland, and some still earn a living by herding reindeer. This Lapp girl is wearing the national dress.

Most people live in towns and cities, which lie mainly in the southern part of these countries. None of them is very big. Denmark's capital, Copenhagen, has a population of about 650,000, and Norway's capital, Oslo, has a population of 760,000. The entire population of Iceland numbers just 277,000.

Caring for the people

The countries of northwestern Europe are prosperous. They earn money from farming, fishing, forestry, and industries. Ships, cars, airplanes, cell phones, and furniture are all manufactured in this region. Norway and Denmark have oil extracted from beneath the North Sea, and Sweden has rich deposits of iron ore, used to make iron and steel.

The countries of northwestern Europe are democracies. Iceland has one of the world's oldest parliaments, the Althing, which traces its history back to A.D. 930 when the island was settled by Norwegian Vikings. Sweden, Norway, and Denmark have royal families, and the monarch of each country is head of state. Denmark, Finland, and Sweden are members of the European Union, but Norway has voted to remain outside.

Scandinavia has a reputation for a high standard of living and for good government-run health care and welfare systems. In the United Nations' Human Development Index—a measurement of standards of living based on national income, education, and health—the five countries of Scandinavia rank among the top 15 nations in the world.

Warm water

It may have a cool climate, but Iceland is a great place for open-air swimming. Geothermal energy heats the water to temperatures as high as 104°F (40°C).

THE BALTIC STATES

Three small countries look out across the Baltic Sea from the coast of northern Europe. Lithuania, Latvia, and Estonia are known as the Baltic States, and for much of the 1900s they were part of the Soviet Union. Since 1991 these small, fiercely patriotic countries have begun to enjoy their first taste of independence for over 50 years.

This part of Europe has always been a battle zone for competing nations, with the bigger Baltic countries such as Finland to the north, Poland to the south, and Russia to the east. Although Lithuania, Latvia, and Estonia broke free from Russia after the Russian Revolution of 1917, the Soviet Union seized them in 1940 and placed them under Communist rule, directed from Moscow. Large numbers of people were killed during this period, and even more were forcibly moved to other parts of the Soviet Union and replaced by Russians, Ukrainians, and Belorussians.

But in 1991, as the Soviet Union crumbled, Lithuania, Latvia, and Estonia all declared their independence. This has allowed them to reopen their relationships with surrounding countries, particularly Sweden and Finland, on the other side of the Baltic Sea and to trade with the rest of Europe.

Folk tradition

This Latvian girl is wearing traditional folk dress and playing a percussion instrument. Folk music and folktales are a central part of Latvian culture.

Changing times

Folktales and legends play a large role in the cultures of the Baltic States—as do music, theater, and dance. The summer festivals in the towns and villages provide showcases for folksinging and dancing. Latvia in particular is famous for its choirs. Rock music, both imported and homegrown, also has enthusiastic fans.

Although religion was discouraged under Soviet rule, Christianity survived. In Estonia and Latvia most people are Protestants of the Lutheran Church, while in Lithuania the people are fervent Roman Catholics.

Food factories

Food processing is an important industry in the Baltic countries. This woman is preparing fish in an Estonian factory.

The Baltic States are supported by a mixture of farming, forestry, and industries. During the Soviet era huge farms were created, and large-scale industries were introduced. The farms still produce huge quantities of grain, sugar beets, and flax (to make linen), as well as cattle and pigs. The main industries are food processing, electrical engineering, and chemical and timber product manufacturing. Tourism is increasingly important to the region. Old cities, such as Riga, Latvia's capital, are now popular vacation destinations.

THE BRITISH ISLES

The British Isles contain two main islands and two independent nations. The larger island is Great Britain. It consists of England, Scotland, and Wales. West of Great Britain is Ireland, which is divided in half. The southern part of the island is the independent Republic of Ireland. The north is part of the United Kingdom of Great Britain and Northern Ireland.

A crowded land

Great Britain is a crowded island. The total population of the United Kingdom is about 59 million, giving a relatively high population density of 640 people per square mile. But there are still large open spaces, particularly in Scotland. The Republic of Ireland, by contrast, has a total population of just 3.7 million and a population density of 21 people per square mile.

One third of them live in and around the capital, Dublin.

The British Isles have a mild climate with four distinct seasons. The mildness is because of the Gulf Stream, an ocean current that brings warmth from the Caribbean. While it is possible to grow palm trees in sheltered spots in some parts of the west coasts of Ireland and Scotland, parts of Canada on the same latitude suffer long months of icy winters.

Farming is an important industry in both Great Britain and Ireland. Ireland is famous for its dairy herds, producing milk, butter, and cheese and is called the "Emerald Isle" because of its rich, green pastures.

Only one percent of Britons, however, work in agriculture. Nearly 90 percent of the population live in the towns and cities. Great Britain was the first industrial nation in the world, and its factories produce a huge variety of goods. The number of people working in industries has been declining for many decades because other countries can produce goods far more cheaply than Great Britain. Today three fourths of the workforce is employed in service industries such as banking, health care, and tourism.

Open space

Much of Great Britain is built up with towns and cities. But there are some beautiful open spaces such as the Lake District, which is in the northwest of England.

Capital destination

Great Britain's capital, London, is home to the country's parliament. It is also a popular tourist destination, packed with historic sights such as Big Ben.

Cosmopolitan communities

From the 1400s on, British explorers traveled to all parts of the world. They created a network of trading links and gradually took over other countries as colonies in southern Asia, the Far East, the Americas, and Africa. By the end of the 1800s Great Britain ruled over one fourth of the world.

Almost all of these countries are now independent, but links with Great Britain remain. When Great Britain needed more people for its workforce, it encouraged families from the old colonies to emigrate. Today, Great Britain's cities are home to large immigrant communities such as Indian, Pakistani, Afro-Caribbean, Chinese, and Bangladeshi.

The Republic of Ireland was ruled by Great Britain until the 1920s. In the past many Irish people emigrated to other countries to escape poverty. But Ireland's growing economy means it now has to recruit workers from overseas.

Marching past

Pageantry and tradition are an important part of British culture. The Edinburgh Tattoo is an annual Scottish military festival.

Mixed society

British cities are very multicultural. Schoolchildren learn about the different cultures and religions of their classmates.

Church and culture

Great Britain is mainly a secular (nonreligious) society. Although the majority of people are Christian, church attendance is low. Immigrant communities have brought with them their own religions such as Islam and Hinduism. In contrast to Great Britain the Republic of Ireland is strongly Roman Catholic. In Northern Ireland a bitter dispute between the Protestant majority, loyal to Great Britain, and the Roman Catholic minority, who want Northern Ireland to be reunited with the Republic of Ireland, has led to violent confrontation lasting over 30 years.

British and Irish culture is a balancing act between preserving a rich heritage and breaking new boundaries. The country is dotted with old

Industrial town

During the Industrial Revolution in the 1800s northern cities, such as Newcastle, grew in size. This area now suffers from high unemployment.

castles and grand country homes, and Great Britain's royal family and pageantry play a part in state occasions. Local traditions are preserved in each segment of the British Isles. The Scots wear kilts on formal occasions, and the Welsh and the Irish have preserved their old languages. The British are also enthusiastic supporters of the sports they invented, including soccer, rugby, and cricket. But the British Isles look to the future. Great Britain is at the cutting edge of fashion, art, and music, and Ireland's booming technology-based economy has earned it the nickname "Celtic Tiger."

FRANCE

Stretching from the North Sea and the Atlantic Ocean to the warm Mediterranean Sea in the south, France is the largest country in western Europe. It is a leading industrial power and one of the world's most popular tourist destinations. The country is famous for its culture and cuisine, and its capital, Paris, is home to many fine art galleries and restaurants.

Industry with style

Passengers on France's high-speed TGV trains can gaze out over the landscape to medieval castles and ancient cities still crowned with their cathedrals' spires. But France represents a balance between the traditions of the past and the modern world. For example, glass pyramids at the cutting edge of modern architecture have been constructed in the Louvre in Paris. Once a royal palace, the Louvre is now home to paintings and sculptures.

France has a number of major international industries such as car manufacturers Renault, Citroën, and Peugeot. But in France industry and style often go hand in hand. The country's fashion houses and perfumes are famous around the world.

French culture

France is a republic led by a president and a prime minister. Deputies are elected to represent voters in the national parliament in Paris.

In towns and villages, however, the mayor plays an important role. France is also a member of the European Union, and its currency is the euro.

One of the great concerns of all levels of French government is to protect and preserve French culture, from its grand traditions of theater, literature, and art, its great cathedrals and galleries, to daily life in the towns and villages. French culture also thrives on the fact that it is very cosmopolitan.

France once had a large empire. It still has territories in the Caribbean and the South Pacific. People from its former colonies have come to live in France. These people include a large population from northern Africa, particularly Algeria. There are also numerous immigrants from other European countries, notably Portugal, Italy, and Spain.

Eating out

In the summer French restaurants and cafés have tables and chairs on the sidewalk so that families can enjoy dining in the sunshine.

The Louvre

Millions of tourists visit the Louvre in Paris every year. It is home to the world's most famous painting— Leonardo da Vinci's Mona Lisa.

Growing grapes

There are vineyards all over the French countryside. Grapes are cultivated and harvested to make France's famous wines.

Preserving the past

These girls are dressed in regional costumes. As part of their school studies children learn about French history, language, and literature.

Fine cuisine

Eating well is an important part of daily life in France. The French pride themselves on the high standard of the food in their markets and their many restaurants. Patés and cold meats, bread and cakes (patisserie), fresh vegetables, and fruit are commonly eaten. Other French delicacies include frogs' legs and edible snails (escargot). The great interest in eating explains the huge variety of food on sale. There are at least 300 different types of French cheeses alone. This far outstrips the number of cheeses produced by any other country.

France has plenty of good, fertile land, and it also has a range of climates, from hot and sunny in the south to cool and wet in the north. This allows the French to grow their own warm-weather crops such as eggplant, tomatoes, olives, and sunflowers, as well as cool-weather vegetables and fruit such as cabbages and apples. The conditions in much of France are perfect for growing grapes to make their famous wines.

Local loyalties

The French themselves identify strongly with the regions that they come from, which vary from the sun-drenched, hilly landscape of Provence in the south to the green fields and orchards of Normandy in the north. Some regions even have their own languages, notably Brittany in the northwest and the island of Corsica in the Mediterranean.

The dynamic mix of food, climate, landscape, and history have made France an attractive tourist destination. In fact France receives more foreign visitors than any other nation—over 70 million every year—more than the population of France itself.

GERMANY

For much of the last century Germany was divided into democratic West Germany and Communist East Germany. In 1990 the two halves were reunited, giving Germany the highest population of any European country—83 million citizens. Germany is also one of Europe's most successful countries, famous for the very high quality of its industrial products.

Germany's coastlines are bordered by the North and the Baltic seas. Goods being shipped to and from all parts of the world go through major trading ports such as Hamburg and Bremerhaven. They are linked to inland European cities by trucks and freight trains. Germany's main industrial center is the Ruhr Valley in the northwest. The large quantities of coal mined in this region fed the factories in the past, turning iron and steel into heavy machinery and railroad engines. These heavy industries have largely disappeared, and today Germany produces cars, domestic appliances, computers, and telecommunications equipment.

Although less than two percent of Germans work in agriculture, much of Germany remains rural. The rolling landscape is covered by farms and large areas of woodland such as the Black Forest in the southwest. Pig farming is an important industry, and pork plays a large part in German cooking. A favorite snack is wurst—a large, hot sausage, usually bought from a small roadside stall and eaten with a roll and mustard.

High-rise city

Frankfurt is Germany's financial center. Much of the city was flattened by bombs during World War II, and since then towering skyscrapers have been built.

The Länder

Germany was once a collection of small states, many of them ruled by princes and bishops, until they were persuaded in 1871 to join together to form one nation. This process, called unification, created a centralized government.

Germany is still divided into Länder (states), but now representatives from the various parts of the country meet in the parliament, called the Reichstag, in Berlin. The head of the national government is the chancellor, and there is also a president, who acts as the head of state.

Each of the Länder has its own proud traditions. For example, many people still keep a set of traditional costumes to wear at the many local festivals held each year to celebrate the harvest, wine, beer, local legends, or saints. There are also many regional music festivals. Germany was the birthplace of many of the great composers, including Johann Sebastian Bach, Ludwig van Beethoven, and Richard Wagner.

But Germany is a modern nation with a large number of immigrant communities—they make up nine percent of the population. Many of them, notably from Turkey and the Union of Serbia and Montenegro (formerly Yugoslavia), arrived originally to work in the factories.

Most Germans are Protestant Christians, although Germany is an increasingly secular (nonreligious) society. The Länder of Bavaria in southern Germany is mainly Roman Catholic, and there are sizeable Muslim and Jewish communities, particularly in the cities.

Reunification

Germany has gone through a huge and sudden change over the past decade at the end of a traumatic 1900s. In 1900 Germany ruled a large empire with colonies in various parts of the world, but it lost all of these after its defeat in World War I. Economic turmoil in the 1920s and 1930s made people desperate for change, a situation exploited by Adolf Hitler and his Nazi party, who came to power in 1933. Their grand ambitions to conquer a new empire in Europe led to World War II. After six years of war and the mass destruction of German cities Germany was defeated.

The country was divided into two parts—East Germany and West Germany.

For 45 years Germany was ruled as a divided nation, with a heavily patrolled border and fence (part of the so-called "Iron Curtain") running between the two. West Germany prospered as part of Western Europe. East Germany was part of the Soviet empire and was ruled as a Communist state, with few personal freedoms. Although highly productive, its factories were old-fashioned, and its people remained relatively poor.

The collapse of the Soviet empire began in Germany. On an exciting and unforgettable night in November 1989, for the first time in 28 years, East Germans were allowed to cross the frontier that divided the city of Berlin. Eight months later, in 1990, Germany was officially reunited as one country. Berlin became the capital again, and a huge rebuilding program began.

There was a huge gap in living standards between East Germany and West Germany and, after 45 years of separation, considerable differences in attitudes, which are taking time to resolve. But Germany remains Europe's leading industrial nation. A key member of the European Union, it has abandoned its former currency in favor of the euro.

The Berlin Wall

In 1961 the Communist government of East Germany built a huge wall across Berlin to separate it from the West. In 1989 mass demonstrations led to the government's collapse, and the wall was torn down.

Local traditions

Traditional festivals and fairs are held in towns and villages throughout Germany. The streets are decorated with flags and flower displays, and crowds gather to enjoy the dancing and music.

THE LOW COUNTRIES

The set of nations known as the Low Countries— the Netherlands, Belgium, and Luxembourg—are called this because, in general, they do not rise high above sea level. In fact more than one third of the Netherlands is below sea level because over the centuries farmland has been reclaimed from marshes and the sea by building dikes (sea walls) and canals.

Although each is now independent, the Low Countries are linked together by history. Around 500 years ago they all belonged to Spain. Today all three countries are democracies with elected parliaments, and all three have ruling royal families—Belgium has a king, the Netherlands has a queen, and Luxembourg has a grand duke. Belgium has three languages. In the northern part, which is called Flanders, the people speak Dutch— similar to the Dutch spoken in the Netherlands. The people in the southern part of the country, called the Walloons, speak French. There are also German-speaking people in the east of the country. The people of Luxembourg speak French, German, and their own language, Letzebuergesch. All three nations have sizable immigrant communities located mainly in the cosmopolitan cities.

Trading nations

The Low Countries are prosperous. Luxembourg has the highest gross domestic product (GDP—a way of judging the wealth of a country) per head per year in the world. All three countries rank among the top 15 nations in the United Nations' Human Development Index— a measurement of quality of life.

They have a history of trade going back centuries. This provided the money to build great trading centers such as the Dutch cities of Amsterdam (the capital of the Netherlands) and Delft and the Belgian cities of Ghent and Bruges. Today these represent a curious blend between old and new. Among the old churches and elegant medieval mansions and guild houses are modern shopping malls and offices.

The Dutch prefer their bicycles to their cars, and most cities in the Netherlands have carefully planned cycle paths.

Both the Netherlands and Belgium are major industrial countries, producing cars, domestic appliances, textiles, and petrochemicals. Luxembourg is a financial center for banking, investment, and insurance. Brussels, Belgium's main city, is called the "capital of Europe" because many of the most important offices of the European Union are based there.

The Netherlands has one of the highest population densities in Europe, with about 156 people per square mile. Many live in the central ring of cities called the Randstad, including Rotterdam, Amsterdam, and The Hague. These are in the provinces of North Holland and South Holland, which have given rise to the other name for the Netherlands—Holland.

European center

The Belgian capital, Brussels, is home to the European Parliament— a directly elected forum for the European Union. Elections are held every five years.

Wind power

Much of the Netherlands is land reclaimed from the sea. Windmills were used to pump water from the land. Today wind turbines are used to generate electricity.

Tulips and chocolates

Farming plays an important role in the Low Countries. The Netherlands is famous for its dairy farms. Cattle are raised on the rich grass of the polders (reclaimed land from the sea), and their milk is made into cheeses such as Edam and Gouda. Windmills are used to pump water out of the polders and into the canals, although modern pumps do most of the work these days. The polders of the west coast are used to grow flower bulbs. Millions of tulips, daffodils, and other flowers are sold every day of the week at Aalsmeer, the world's largest flower market. Another symbol of the Netherlands is wooden clogs, which some people still wear to protect their feet from the mud and wet ground.

Belgium is famous for its chocolates, beer, waffles, and french fries, which are crispy and eaten with mayonnaise. It also has some of the best restaurants in Europe. Good food plays a central role in Belgian life.

The Dutch love seafood. One popular local delicacy is herring. It is cured in brine and eaten raw—held by the tail and dropped into the mouth whole.

Flower power
Tulip growing has been a major business for the Netherlands since the 1600s. Every year about three billion tulip bulbs are produced in the country.

Big cheese
Every week the Dutch town of Alkmaar holds a traditional cheese market. The porters carry cheese on barrows suspended from their shoulders.

THE IBERIAN PENINSULA

The great square-shaped piece of land at the southwestern corner of Europe is named after the Iberians, the people who lived there in ancient times before the Romans conquered the area in the 100s B.C. Today the Iberian Peninsula consists of two countries, Spain and Portugal.

Spain occupies the bigger part of the peninsula, making it the second largest country in Western Europe after France. Its Atlantic coast in the north has a cool climate with plenty of rain, which keeps the countryside green almost all year. In the northeast the land rises up into a high ridge of rugged mountains, the Pyrenees, which form a natural frontier with France. In the mountains, sandwiched between the borders of Spain and France, lies the tiny independent state of Andorra—a country of sheep fields, valley farms, and ski resorts that are popular with tourists.

Living with the heat

Most of Spain, however, is a hot and dry plateau. To the south and east lies the Mediterranean Sea with its long, sandy beaches and strings of summer vacation resorts. The tourist industry is very important to the Spanish economy, as is agriculture. The hot climate is good for growing tomatoes, fruits, olives, and grapes for wine.

During the summer many people escape the heat of the day by taking a siesta (a long nap after a light lunch) before returning to work in the late afternoon. The main meal of the day is in the evening. It can be grilled meat, or a hearty stew of beans, vegetables, meat, and sausage, or perhaps the famous Spanish dish of paella, made of saffron-flavored rice cooked with shrimp, shellfish, chicken, and ham. Spanish restaurants often serve tapas (plates of tasty snacks such as cold meats, olives, and meatballs).

Fishy dish

Paella is Spain's most famous dish. The rice-based speciality contains morsels of seafood, meat, and vegetables. Every region of Spain has its own distinct method of preparation.

Regional Spain

Spain is divided into regions with contrasting cultures. The Basque country in the north has its own language, which is very different from Spanish. Catalonia, on the northeast coast, also has its own language, and it is the main language of Andorra. Asturias on the northern Atlantic coast is green and mountainous. Andalucía in the south is hot and dry and covered with rocky hills. This last place is home to the fiery gypsy flamenco dance, performed to the rhythms of the guitar—an instrument that is associated with Spain.

Trying to hold together this diverse nation has caused problems in the past. In 1936–1939 there was a civil war, which resulted in victory for the dictator General Francisco Franco. Shortly after his death in 1975 democracy was restored under King Juan Carlos. Since then Spain has undergone rapid development, and its cities have become more modern.

Fiestas and bullfights

Fiestas (festivals) are often held to celebrate a local saint—reflecting the fact that most Spaniards are Roman Catholics. Fiestas are colorful events with traditional costumes, fairs, fireworks, and parades.

Many towns and cities have bullrings where bullfighting takes place. They are large, round buildings with an open arena inside. The matadors (bullfighters) subdue the bulls with powerful darts and kill them with a single thrust of a sword. The Portuguese also have bullfights, but they are conducted on horseback by a *cavaleiro*. Horse and rider perform dainty maneuvers to control the bull, which is not killed in the ring.

Modern museum

The Guggenheim Museum in the Spanish city of Bilbao is home to famous works of art. The building is made from titanium and glass.

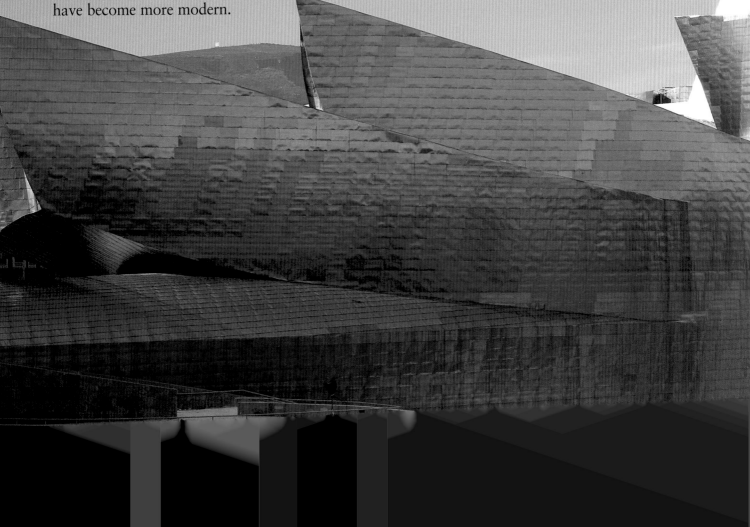

Collecting cork

Cork is usually harvested in August. The heat causes the cork layer to pull away, making it is easier to remove from the tree.

The far west of Europe

Portugal may be attached to Spain by a long border, but it has its own special character. The coasts of Portugal look out over the Atlantic. They are cool and misty in the north, creating a green landscape called the Costa Verde (Green Coast), but they are warmer and sunnier in the Algarve province of the south. The whitewashed towns of the Algarve are a popular destination for tourists. In the hills and mountains along the border with Spain are cork-oak forests. Bark is stripped off the trees to make bottle corks.

Fishing is an important industry in both Spain and Portugal. Vigo in northeastern Spain is Europe's biggest fishing port, and fish plays a central role in Portuguese cooking. *Bacalhau* is a tangy stew made with salt cod, and in the summer the streets of Lisbon, the Portuguese capital, are scented with the smell of grilled sardines cooked on street barbecues.

ITALY AND ITS NEIGHBORS

B oot-shaped Italy kicks out into the Mediterranean Sea. Its streets, piazzas (squares), and monuments are full of reminders of its historic past. For centuries it was the heart of an ancient empire that stretched across Europe, and later it was home to Renaissance art and culture. Today it is a vibrant, modern nation and a world leader in fashion and style.

Regional differences

Traditionally Italy is divided in half—the cooler, more industrial and wealthier north and the hotter, drier, and poorer south. The capital, Rome, is in the middle. Italy also has two large islands—Sicily and Sardinia.

During medieval times Italy was divided into numerous small, independent states, centering on magnificent cities, such as Florence, Venice, and Milan, with their cathedrals, palaces, and splendid collections of art. These small states were only brought together as one country in 1861.

Traditionally Italians have identified strongly with the town or region where they were born. They see themselves first as Genoan, Tuscan, or Sicilian and second as Italian. Each area has not only its distinctive dialect or accent but also its own kinds of cooking and brands of coffee and wine. Naples, for example, is famed for its pizzas and Parma for its cured ham.

The towns and cities are very proud of their identities and histories. Most towns hold a festival in the summer when leading national or international musicians, opera singers, and rock stars are invited to perform. Even small villages hold a *sagra* (an outdoor summer feast), where the local food speciality is served at long trestle tables and the whole community dances to the music of a local rock band. Even on ordinary days there is a festive air in many towns in the early evening, especially in the summer when people walk in the streets, shop, chat, and drink in cafés—a custom called the *passeggiata*.

Cars and clothes

Agriculture has always been an important industry in Italy, and the country still has many farming communities. However, one third of the labor force now works in manufacturing, and Italy is known for the design flair of its commercial products. It is home to famous car manufacturers, such as Fiat and Ferrari, and fashion designers such as Armani and Versace. However, most people work in service industries such as banking and tourism.

Floating city

The city of Venice has more
than 150 canals running
through it. The waterways
bustle with waterbuses,
barges, and gondolas.
Thousands of tourists
flock to the city
every year.

Tomato harvest

The Italian climate is ideal for
growing tomatoes. Tomatoes
originated in South America,
and European explorers
brought them to Italy
in the 1500s.

magnificent museums. In fact Vatican City's many priceless art treasures make it, per square yard, one of the richest countries in the world.

The independent republic of San Marino, just 24 sq. mi. (67 sq km), also lies within Italy. Over half of its income is generated by tourism. The wealthy independent principality of Monaco (0.74 sq. mi./1.9 sq km) lies on the Mediterranean coast just beyond the border with France. It is famed for its glamor and casinos.

Another small state south of Italy is Malta. Its two main islands lie in the middle of a channel in the Mediterranean Sea, separating Italy from Africa. The Romans, Arabs, Normans, Spanish, French, and English have all ruled Malta, each leaving traces in the nation's rich mix of cultures. It became an independent nation in 1964 and now seeks European Union membership.

Pasta popularity

Pasta, of course, is Italy's best-known dish. A dough made with durum wheat flour, it comes in at least 200 different shapes and sizes. The Italians eat a great deal of pasta. It is usually served with a sauce such as garlic fried in olive oil with chili or homemade tomato sauce. Every household has its own recipe for tomato sauce, cooked and bottled each summer.

Small states

Lying in the heart of Rome is Vatican City—the world's smallest independent state and the headquarters of the Roman Catholic Church. Less than half a square mile in size, it has about 1,000 inhabitants, including the Pope (the head of the Roman Catholic Church), and it contains St. Peter's Basilica, the Papal Palace, and a host of

Religious leader

Vatican City is home to the Pope, the head of the Roman Catholic Church. Millions of pilgrims visit the Vatican every year to hear Pope John Paul II lead prayers.

CENTRAL EUROPE

The band of countries that runs across central Europe reaches to the Baltic Sea in the north, where icy winds blow in the winter. In the south lies Greece, where the summers are long and hot. The landlocked countries in the middle rise up into mountains—the Carpathian and Tatra Mountains in Poland and Slovakia and the Alps in Austria, Switzerland, and Slovenia.

Goulash and Gruyère

In the flat plains of central Poland—a land of lakes and forests and medieval castles—farmers grow wheat, rye, potatoes, and sugar beets. Hungary is warm enough to grow large quantities of peppers. Dried and powdered, they are used to make paprika, a key ingredient of the national dish goulash (a stew). In Greece farmers grow olives, lemons, grapes, and sunflowers.

Large areas of the mountains are forested, and timber is an important export of Austria and Slovenia. The valleys trap the summer warmth, allowing a wide range of fruits and vegetables can grow. Grapes for wine grow high in the Swiss mountains on sheltered, south-facing terraces. Mountain farmers tend cattle and sheep. Cows' milk is used to make cheese, such as Swiss Gruyère and Emmental, which can be heated in a pot to make fondue (a melted cheese dip).

Mountain land

Over 60 percent of Switzerland is mountainous. The Alps occupy the central and southern regions of the country and are home to many ski resorts.

Two paths

Events in recent history divided the countries of central Europe into two groups—communist and noncommunist. After the end of World War II in 1945 Communist governments took over in Poland, Hungary, and Czechoslovakia and came under the control of the Soviet Union. In 1989 as the Soviet Union collapsed they declared their independence. Czechoslovakia split into two countries— the Czech Republic and Slovakia—in 1993.

Independence has given these countries a new opportunity to find their true identities. Each has its own distinct character and language. But they are struggling to rebuild their economies, switching from heavy industries and mining to modern industries, making cars, domestic appliances and other consumer goods, computers, and telecommunications equipment. In 1999 Poland, the Czech Republic, and Hungary joined NATO (the military alliance of Western nations), and they have applied to join the

Fun on the slopes

The mountains of central Europe are home to many popular ski resorts. This young boy is traveling up a slope on a ski lift in an Austrian resort.

European Union. But they still lag behind Western Europe. For example, the economy of the Western European nation of France is around 30 times stronger than that of Hungary.

Austria managed to escape being taken over by the Soviet Union and has prospered as a member of the European Union. It produces iron, steel, textiles, and machinery and has more organic farmers than any other nation in Europe. Tourism is an important industry. In the summer boats take visitors down the Danube River to Vienna, the grand old capital of the Austrian empire—a city of palaces, elegant coffeehouses, and music. In the winter skiers and other winter sports enthusiasts flock to the mountain ski resorts.

Switzerland is a neutral country and was not directly involved with either of the world wars, although it has a large and active citizens' army, trained and ready to defend it. Like Austria, it has plenty of ski resorts, but it also earns income from banking and from manufacturing medicines and its famous watches.

The Austrians speak German and so do the majority of the Swiss. But Switzerland is a multilingual land—one-fifth speak French, and minorities speak Italian or a language called Romansch, which is related to Latin.

Nestling between Austria and Switzerland is the tiny German-speaking principality of Liechtenstein. It has an area of about 62 sq. mi. (160 sq km) and a population of just 32,000. A small industrial country, it also earns a high income from banking.

Romany dance

There is a sizeable gypsy population in central Europe. This gypsy girl from the Czech Republic is performing a traditional folk dance.

The Balkans

The area of land from the south of Austria down to the Mediterranean Sea is known as the Balkans. For centuries it was the crossroads and battleground between the Muslim Turks and Christian Europe. After World War II Communist leader Marshal Tito ruled over the united country of Yugoslavia (now the Union of Serbia and Montenegro). He recognized the divisions in his land and once said: "I am the leader of one country, which has two alphabets, three languages, four religions, and five nationalities."

Tourism trade

Croatia has managed to rebuild its tourist industry after the war in the 1990s. Its warm climate, beaches, and medieval towns make it a popular destination.

Tito died in 1980, and not long after, the historic stresses and strains began to show. When Serbia attempted to dominate the other republics in the early 1990s, Slovenia, Croatia, and Bosnia-Herzegovina declared independence, and Macedonia followed in 1991. A bloody civil war broke out, first in Croatia and then in Bosnia, between Christian Serbs and the Bosnian Muslims before an uneasy peace was imposed in 1995 with the help of NATO forces. In 1998

the Serbs tried to take control of Kosovo, home to Albanian Muslims, and were forcibly removed by NATO the following year.

These troubles have caused a great deal of difficulty for these countries. Slovenia has been least affected, however, and is enjoying rapid economic progress manufacturing cars, medicines, chemicals, and telecommunications products and developing winter sports and summer tourist facilities. Croatia is beginning to welcome back tourists, who come to visit the beaches and historic towns, such as Dubrovnik, and to sail among the many islands of the Dalmatian coast.

Albania was under Communist rule until 1992. It has recently been through a troubled period verging on civil war. Thousands of desperate Albanians fled in boats across the Adriatic Sea to Italy. Most of the Albanians who stayed behind are farmers, herding sheep, goats, and cattle and growing vegetables. Albania is the poorest country in Europe, but there are signs that the economy is beginning to recover, with private ownership encouraged.

Nod for "no"

This Albanian family is dressed in traditional costumes for a festival. One Albanian custom often confuses visitors—they shake their heads for "yes" and nod their heads for "no."

The sun-drenched south

Greece, at the southern tip of central Europe, watched nervously as its northern neighbors descended into chaos. By contrast, it has prospered as a member of the European Union and has adopted the euro currency.

Over 2,500 years ago Greece ruled much of the eastern Mediterranean and created the first great European civilization. The Greeks were noted as adventurous traders and sailors and still own the fourth largest shipping fleet in the world. Numerous ships are needed to ferry goods and people around the many Greek islands in the Mediterranean—dry, rocky lumps of land dotted with whitewashed villages and crowned with the domes of ancient churches.

Greek Christians belong mainly to the Orthodox Church, which has developed along a separate path from the Roman Catholic Church since 1054. Stylized portrait paintings, called icons, depicting saints and characters from the Bible, play a central role in worship.

For thousands of years people have survived on the Greek islands by fishing and farming.

Painted icons
The walls of Greek Orthodox churches are often covered in iconic paintings of saints and biblical figures.

Today tourism brings in much needed extra income. Tourists stay in small hotels and eat at local tavernas (restaurants) where traditional dishes are served such as lamb kababs, goat cheese, and moussaka (a dish made of minced lamb, potatoes, tomatoes, and eggplant). Tourists also visit mainland Greece to see the ancient sites such as the Parthenon on the Acropolis in Athens. There are 10.6 million people living in Greece, and one third live in and around Athens, the capital. The mixture of heat and dense traffic has made this one of the most polluted cities on earth, putting the ancient stone of the Acropolis under threat.

The Acropolis
The Acropolis dominates Athen's skyline. It houses the remains of ancient Greek temples over 2,500 years old. The columns of the Parthenon temple still stand today.

EASTERN EUROPE

Until 1989 the countries of Eastern Europe were part of the Soviet Union. Now they are independent, but many of them still consider themselves to have more in common with Russia than with the rest of Europe. Their economies are struggling to adapt after years of Soviet rule, and many countries in the region face an uncertain future.

Agriculture and industry

The Ukraine is one of Europe's largest countries. On its wide, grassy plains farmers grow wheat, barley, sugar beets, and cotton and rear cattle and pigs. Coal is mined in large quantities in the Donets Basin in eastern Ukraine, fueling industries that make steel, machinery, and ships. Factories also produce chemicals and processed food. To the south lie the sunny coasts of the Black Sea and the large, diamond-shaped peninsula called the Crimea, which has a number of popular beach resorts. Over two thirds of the population live in cities. Like many of the towns and cities of the old Soviet empire, they are dominated by large apartment blocks and offices. Russian was widely spoken during the Soviet era, but Ukrainian became the official language again in 1991.

Farm work

Although farm production is largely mechanized, some farmers still take their produce to the market in horse-drawn carts.

Nuclear legacy

The Ukraine is haunted by a tragic legacy of Soviet rule. In 1986 a nuclear power plant at Chernobyl to the north of the city of Kiev exploded, spilling radioactive waste into the air and poisoning a vast area of farmland. It killed 31 people immediately, but some 25,000 people have since died from illnesses, such as cancer, caused by the radioactive fallout. It is the worst nuclear accident on record.

Dracula and roses

Romania was ruled for 25 years by a communist dictator named Nicolae Ceausescu. One of his most unpopular policies was to create huge farms by destroying 7,000 villages. In 1989 he was overthrown in a rebellion and executed. The country has been trying to recover from these events by developing its industries, including tourism. The Black Sea coast is popular in the summer. Walkers can explore the beautiful Carpathian Mountains and the Transylvania Alps—the home, according to legends, of vampires. Bran Castle is said to be the castle of the original Count Dracula. Romania also has winter sports resorts such as Poiana Brasov in Transylvania.

About two percent of Romanians are gypsies. No one is sure where they came from originally, but they have lived in Romania for over 1,000 years and have spread out to many other parts of Europe. Gypsies speak a language called Romany, but strangely the name has nothing to do with Romania. They are the source of much of the lively violin music and dance traditions of eastern Europe. Despite this, they have suffered a long history of persecution and discrimination, which became more acute after the collapse of communism.

Bulgaria produces grain, fruits, and a range of vegetables on a fertile plain that stretches south from the Danube River to the Balkan Mountains in the middle of the country.

Over 20 percent of the population earn their income from farming—a very high proportion by European standards. Many of them grow roses to make essence of rose, which is used in the perfume industry. Colossal amounts of the flowers are needed—it takes over 6,630 lbs (3,000kg) of rose petals to make one quart of rose oil.

Uncertain future

Moldova has rich, dark soil, which is the basis of its agricultural industry, producing fruits such as apples and grapes, as well as nuts and honey. Over half of the population lives and works on farms, and much of the food is sent to factories in the food-processing industry. Most of the people are Moldovans, who are closely related to Romanians, but there are large minorities of Ukrainians and Russians.

Of all the countries of Eastern Europe, Moldova has suffered the most in the recent political changes and misses the support once given to it by the Soviet Union. Its industries have collapsed, and unemployment is soaring.

Dracula's castle

Despite popular myths, Bran Castle has no historic links with Vlad Tepes, the cruel medieval prince on whom writer Bram Stoker based his Dracula *story. However, its fairy-tale towers make it a popular tourist attraction.*

RUSSIA

Russia is the largest country in the world—
it stretches one third of the way around the
globe. One fourth of the country lies north of the
Arctic Circle, and long, bitterly cold winters are
part of Russian life. It takes seven days to cross Russia on
the Trans-Siberian Railroad, which runs from the capital,
Moscow, to Vladivostok on the Pacific coast.

About one fifth of Russia is in Europe,
and the rest is in Asia. The dividing line is the
Ural Mountains. These form a band running
north to south some 1,240 mi. (2,000km) east
of Russia's capital, Moscow. There is good
farmland in European Russia, especially in the
warmer, southern regions, which reach down to
the Black Sea. Large, government-owned farms
grow grain and fruit and raise cattle. In the
south farmers grow peaches and oranges.

Communist rule

For over 70 years during the 1900s Russia
was ruled by a communist government and
headed a large country called the Soviet Union.
The government owned all land, buildings,
farms, and factories on behalf of all the people.
The Soviet government exerted strict control
over the people, limiting what they could say
and do, as well as where they could go.

For many years the Soviet Union was
involved in a "Cold War" with Western
nations led by the U.S. The West feared
communism, and the two sides developed
nuclear weapons arsenals in case the other
side attacked. This was a huge drain on Soviet
resources. In addition, the lack of industrial
competition in the Soviet Union had led to
an over-bureaucratic and inefficient system,
and the economy of the country began
to crumble during the 1980s.

Wheat harvest

Despite its size, much of Russia lacks the soil and climate for agriculture—it is either too cold or too dry. The fertile land of western Russia is used to grow crops and raise livestock.

The Kremlin

The Kremlin occupies a triangular plot of land in Russia's capital, Moscow. It was the government's power base during the Soviet years.

In 1991 the Communist government collapsed, and the Soviet Union broke up. Many satellite states, such as Kazahkstan, Azerbaijan, and Armenia, demanded independence from Moscow. With Russia, they formed a new group of 12 countries called the Commonwealth of Independent States (CIS). Russia itself is also called the Russian Federation and includes 21 self-governing member republics. Some of these have expressed a desire to be free of Russian control— including the southern republic of Chechnya, where war has raged.

Northern people

The Dolgan people originated in northern Russia and traditionally lived by fishing and hunting reindeer. Under Soviet rule they were forced to work on collective farms.

New opportunities

Since 1991 Russia has been struggling to modernize its economy and to move from a Communist system to a market economy where companies compete for business. This means switching from the old state-run heavy industries, producing coal, steel, ships, machinery, and chemicals, to producing things to export to the rest of the world such as electrical equipment, cameras, and cars. Russia has had some difficult times adjusting, but there are signs that private enterprise is helping the economy to grow again.

In general Russians have welcomed the changes. Under the Communist regime stores had little in them, and products were generally of low quality. Now Russians can buy imported products from all over the world. But the market economy has brought problems.

Under the Soviet regime there was no unemployment—now a sizable part of the workforce is without a job. In addition, the reliable welfare and health care systems have withered away.

Russia has vast natural resources—plenty of oil and natural gas, coal, timber, and metals. Many of these come from the tundra and forests of Siberia in central Russia and are processed by industrial cities such as Omsk and Krasnoyarsk, which lie on the route of the Trans-Siberian Railroad.

Onion domes

Russian churches are famous for their onion-shaped domes. They are painted in bright colors or covered in glittering gold leaf and give Russian cities unique skylines. These star-covered blue domes top the Yuzier Monastery in Moscow.

A mixture of peoples

Russia contains over 100 different peoples.
Russians make up over 80 percent of the
population, but there are also Tartars, Chuvash,
and Bashkir in western (European) Russia,
Nenets in the far north, and Yakuts in Siberia,
to name but a few. Each has their own traditions
and identity. Under the Communists thousands
of people were moved around the country, so
the populations have become very mixed.

Under communism religion was discouraged,
but today people are allowed to worship freely.
The majority of worshipers are Russian
Orthodox Christians, but a sizable minority
are Muslims, especially in the south.

The Russian cities of St. Petersburg and
Moscow rival each other as cultural centers.
They have fine churches, palaces, ballet
schools, art museums, and a great
tradition of music and literature.

Cold north

*In northern Siberia the winters are very cold, with
temperatures plummeting to -40°F (-40°C). Hardy
reindeer are used to pull sleighs along the icy roads.*

Orthodox Church

*Many people in Russia
belong to the Russian
Orthodox Church, a
branch of Christianity.
During the Soviet era
religion was oppressed,
but people now have
religious freedom.*

ALBANIA

Capital
Tirana
Area
10,600 sq. mi.
Population
3,510,484
Population density
332 per sq. mi.
Life expectancy
69 (m); 75 (f)
Religions
Christianity, Islam
Languages
Albanian (dialects: Gheg in north, Tosk in south)
Adult literacy rate
100 percent
Currency
Lek

 ANDORRA

Capital
Andorra la Vella
Area
174 sq. mi.
Population
67,627
Population density
389 per sq. mi.
Life expectancy
80 (m); 87 (f)
Religion
Christianity
Languages
Catalan, French, Castilian
Adult literacy rate
100 percent
Currency
Euro

 AUSTRIA

Capital
Vienna
Area
31,900 sq. mi.
Population
8,150,835
Population density
255 per sq. mi.
Life expectancy
73 (m); 80 (f)
Religion
Christianity
Language
German
Adult literacy rate
100 percent
Currency
Euro

 BELARUS

Capital
Minsk
Area
80,100 sq. mi.
Population
10,350,194
Population density
129 per sq. mi.
Life expectancy
62 (m); 74 (f)
Religion
Christianity
Languages
Belarussian, Russian
Adult literacy rate
98 percent
Currency
Ruble

 BELGIUM

Capital
Brussels
Area
11,700 sq. mi.
Population
10,258,768
Population density
880 sq. mi.
Life expectancy
74 (m); 81 (f)
Religion
Christianity
Languages
Flemish, French, German
Adult literacy rate
99 percent
Currency
Euro

 BOSNIA AND HERZEGOVINA

Capital
Sarajevo
Area
19,700 sq. mi.
Population
3,922,205
Population density
199 per sq. mi.
Life expectancy
69 (m); 75 (f)
Religions
Islam, Christianity
Languages
Serbo-Croat (Muslims and Croats use Roman script; Serbs use Cyrillic)
Adult literacy rate
86 percent
Currency
Mark

BULGARIA

Capital
Sofia
Area
42,600 sq. mi.
Population
7,707,495
Population density
181 per sq. mi.
Life expectancy
68 (m); 75 (f)
Religions
Christianity, Islam
Language
Bulgarian
Adult literacy rate
98 percent
Currency
Lev

 CROATIA

Capital
Zagreb
Area
21,800 sq. mi.
Population
4,334,142
Population density
199 per sq. mi.
Life expectancy
70 (m); 73 (f)
Religion
Christianity
Language
Serbo-Croatian (Roman script)
Adult literacy rate
97 percent
Currency
Kuna

 CZECH REPUBLIC

Capital
Prague
Area
30,300 sq. mi.
Population
10,264,212
Population density
338 per sq. mi.
Life expectancy
71 (m); 78 (f)
Religion
Christianity
Languages
Czech, German, Slovak
Adult literacy rate
99 percent
Currency
Czech koruna

 DENMARK

Capital
Copenhagen
Area
16,300 sq. mi.
Population
5,352,815
Population density
328 per sq. mi.
Life expectancy
74 (m); 79 (f)
Religion
Christianity
Languages
Danish, Faroese
Adult literacy rate
100 percent
Currency
Danish Krone

 ESTONIA

Capital
Tallinn
Area
17,400 sq. mi.
Population
1,423,316
Population density
82 per sq. mi.
Life expectancy
63 (m); 76 (f)
Religion
Christianity
Languages
Estonian, Russian
Adult literacy rate
100 percent
Currency
Kroon

 FINLAND

Capital
Helsinki
Area
117,800 sq. mi.
Population
5,175,783
Population density
44 per sq. mi.
Life expectancy
74 (m); 81 (f)
Religion
Christianity
Languages
Finnish, Swedish
Adult literacy rate
99 percent
Currency
Euro

 **FRANCE**

Capital
Paris
Area
210,400 sq. mi.
Population
59,551,227
Population density
283 per sq. mi.
Life expectancy
75 (m); 83 (f)
Religion
Christianity
Languages
French, Breton, Basque, and several regional dialects
Adult literacy rate
99 percent
Currency
Euro

 GERMANY

Capital
Berlin
Area
135,100 sq. mi.
Population
83,029,536
Population density
615 per sq. mi.
Life expectancy
74 (m); 81 (f)
Religion
Christianity
Language
German
Adult literacy rate
100 percent
Currency
Euro

 **GREECE**

Capital
Athens
Area
50,400 sq. mi.
Population
10,623,835
Population density
211 per sq. mi.
Life expectancy
76 (m); 81 (f)
Religion
Christianity
Languages
Greek, English, French
Adult literacy rate
95 percent
Currency
Euro

French food

France has a reputation for its fine cuisine. Stores, big and small, stock fine patés, cheeses, and patisserie (bread and cakes).

 HUNGARY

Capital
Budapest
Area
35,600 sq. mi.
Population
10,106,107
Population density
284 per sq. mi.
Life expectancy
67 (m); 76 (f)
Religion
Christianity
Language
Hungarian (Magyar)
Adult literacy rate
99 percent
Currency
Forint

Dressing up

Greece has many national traditions, and every region has its own unique one as well.

ICELAND

Capital
Reykjavik
Area
38,700 sq. mi.
Population
277,906
Population density
7 per sq. mi.
Life expectancy
77 (m); 82 (f)
Religion
Christianity
Language
Icelandic (Islenka)
Adult literacy rate
100 percent
Currency
Icelandic krona

IRELAND

Capital
Dublin
Area
26,600 sq. mi.
Population
3,840,838
Population density
145 per sq. mi.
Life expectancy
74 (m); 80 (f)
Religion
Christianity
Languages
Irish (Gaelic), English
Adult literacy rate
100 percent
Currency
Euro

ITALY

Capital
Rome
Area
113,400 sq. mi.
Population
57,679,825
Population density
509 per sq. mi.
Life expectancy
76 (m); 83 (f)
Religion
Christianity
Languages
Italian, German, French, Slovene
Adult literacy rate
97 percent
Currency
Euro

LATVIA

Capital
Riga
Area
24,900 sq. mi.
Population
2,385,321
Population density
96 per sq. mi.
Life expectancy
62 (m); 74 (f)
Religion
Christianity
Languages
Lettish, Lithuanian, Russian
Adult literacy rate
92 percent
Currency
Lat

LIECHTENSTEIN

Capital
Vaduz
Area
60 sq. mi.
Population
32,528
Population density
542 per sq. mi.
Life expectancy
75(m); 81 (f)
Religion
Christianity
Language
German (Alemannic dialect)
Adult literacy rate
100 percent
Currency
Swiss Franc

 LITHUANIA

Capital
Vilnius
Area
25,100 sq. mi.
Population
3,610,535
Population density
144 per sq. mi.
Life expectancy
63 (m); 75 (f)
Religion
Christianity
Languages
Lithuanian, Polish, Russian
Adult literacy rate
98 percent
Currency
Litas

LUXEMBOURG

Capital
Luxembourg
Area
1,00 sq. mi.
Population
442,972
Population density
444 per sq. mi.
Life expectancy
74 (m); 81 (f)
Religion
Christianity
Languages
Luxembourgian, French, German, English
Adult literacy rate
100 percent
Currency
Euro

 **MACEDONIA**

Capital
Skopje
Area
9,900 sq. mi.
Population
2,046,209
Population density
206 per sq. mi.
Life expectancy
72 (m); 76 (f)
Religions
Christianity, Islam
Languages
Macedonian, Albanian, Serbo-Croatian (Cyrillic script)
Adult literacy rate
89 percent
Currency
Macedonian Denar

 MALTA

Capital
Valletta
Area
120 sq. mi.
Population
394,583
Population density
3,228 per sq. mi.
Life expectancy
76 (m); 81 (f)
Religion
Christianity
Languages
Maltese, English
Adult literacy rate
91 percent
Currency
Maltese Lira

 MOLDOVA

Capital
Chisinau
Area
13,000 sq. mi.
Population
4,431,570
Population density
341 per sq. mi.
Life expectancy
60 (m); 69 (f)
Religion
Christianity
Languages
Moldovan, Russian
Adult literacy rate
96 percent
Currency
Moldovan Leu

MONACO

Capital
Monaco-ville
Area
0.75 sq. mi.
Population
31,842
Population density
42,458 per sq. mi.
Life expectancy
75 (m); 83 (f)
Religion
Christianity
Languages
French, Monegasque, Italian
Adult literacy rate
99 percent
Currency
Euro

 NETHERLANDS

Capital
Amsterdam
Area
13,100 sq. mi.
Population
15,981,472
Population density
1,221 per sq. mi.
Life expectancy
76 (m); 81 (f)
Religion
Christianity
Language
Dutch
Adult literacy rate
100 percent
Currency
Euro

 NORWAY

Capital
Oslo
Area
118,700 sq. mi.
Population
4,503,440
Population density
38 per sq. mi.
Life expectancy
76 (m); 83 (f)
Religion
Christianity
Language
Norwegian
Adult literacy rate
100 percent
Currency
Norwegian Krone

Waterways

Amsterdam, the capital of the Netherlands in northern Europe, has 160 canals running through it and over 1,200 bridges.

 POLAND

Capital
Warsaw
Area
117,400 sq. mi.
Population
38,633,912
Population density
329 per sq. mi.
Life expectancy
69 (m); 78 (f)
Religion
Christianity
Language
Polish
Adult literacy rate
99 percent
Currency
Zloty

PORTUGAL

Capital
Lisbon
Area
35,300 sq. mi.
Population
10,066,253
Population density
285 per sq. mi.
Life expectancy
72 (m); 80 (f)
Religion
Christianity
Language
Portuguese
Adult literacy rate
90 percent
Currency
Euro

 ROMANIA

Capital
Bucharest
Area
88,800 sq. mi.
Population
22,364,022
Population density
252 per sq. mi.
Life expectancy
66 (m); 74(f)
Religion
Christianity
Languages
Romanian, Hungarian,
German
Adult literacy rate
97 percent
Currency
Romanian leu

 RUSSIA

Capital
Moscow
Area
6,585,000 sq. mi.
Population
145,470,197
Population density
22 per sq. mi.
Life expectancy
62 (m); 73 (f)
Religions
Christianity, Islam, Judaism
Languages
Russian, Tatar, Yakut,
Chuvash, Bashkir, and others
Adult literacy rate
99 percent
Currency
Ruble

 SAN MARINO

Capital
San Marino
Area
20 sq. mi.
Population
27,336
Population density
1,367 per sq. mi.
Life expectancy
78 (m); 85 (f)
Religion
Christianity
Language
Italian
Adult literacy rate
99 percent
Currency
Euro

 SLOVAKIA

Capital
Bratislava
Area
18,800 sq. mi.
Population
5,414,937
Population density
288 per sq. mi.
Life expectancy
70 (m); 79 (f)
Religion
Christianity
Languages
Slovak, Hungarian
Adult literacy rate
100 percent
Currency
Slovak koruna

 SLOVENIA

Capital
Ljubljana
Area
7,800 sq. mi.
Population
1,930,132
Population density
247 per sq. mi.
Life expectancy
71 (m); 79 (f)
Religion
Christianity
Languages
Slovene, Serbo-Croatian
(Roman script)
Adult literacy rate
99 percent
Currency
Tolar

SPAIN

Capital
Madrid
Area
192,600 sq. mi.
Population
40,037,995
Population density
208 per sq. mi.
Life expectancy
75 (m); 81 (f)
Religion
Christianity
Languages
Spanish (Castilian), Catalan, Galician, Basque
Adult literacy rate
97 percent
Currency
Euro

Fair frills

This man is a wearing traditional costume for a fair in Andalucia in Spain. This region is home to flamenco music and dance.

SWEDEN

Capital
Stockholm
Area
158,700 sq. mi.
Population
8,875,053
Population density
56 per sq. mi.
Life expectancy
77 (m); 81 (f)
Religion
Christianity
Language
Swedish
Adult literacy rate
100 percent
Currency
Swedish krona

SWITZERLAND
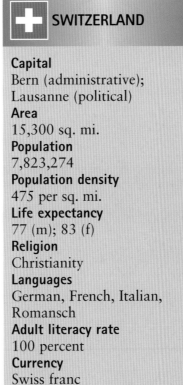

Capital
Bern (administrative);
Lausanne (political)
Area
15,300 sq. mi.
Population
7,823,274
Population density
475 per sq. mi.
Life expectancy
77 (m); 83 (f)
Religion
Christianity
Languages
German, French, Italian, Romansch
Adult literacy rate
100 percent
Currency
Swiss franc

UKRAINE

Capital
Kiev
Area
232,800 sq. mi.
Population
48,760,474
Population density
209 per sq. mi.
Life expectancy
61 (m); 72 (f)
Religion
Christianity
Languages
Ukrainian, Russian
Adult literacy rate
99 percent
Currency
Hryvnya

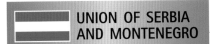
UNION OF SERBIA AND MONTENEGRO

Capital
Belgrade
Area
39,400 sq. mi.
Population
10,677,290
Population density
271 per sq. mi.
Life expectancy
71 (m); 77 (f)
Religions
Christianity, Islam
Language
Serbo-Croatian (Cyrillic script)
Adult literacy rate
98 percent
Currency
Yugoslav new dinar

UNITED KINGDOM

Capital
London
Area
93,200 sq. mi.
Population
59,647,790
Population density
640 per sq. mi.
Life expectancy
75 (m); 81 (f)
Religions
Christianity, Islam
Languages
English, Welsh, Scottish, Gaelic
Adult literacy rate
100 percent
Currency
Pound sterling

VATICAN CITY

Area
108.7 acres
Population
870
Population density
5,000 per sq. mi.
Life expectancy
74 (m); 80 (f)
Religion
Christianity
Languages
Italian, Latin
Adult literacy rate
100 percent
Currency
Euro

Rural appeal

Although most people in the United Kingdom live in towns and cities there are also large areas of beautiful, green countryside such as Somerset and Dorest.

The United States of America

Canada

Mexico

The Caribbean

Central America

NORTH AMERICA

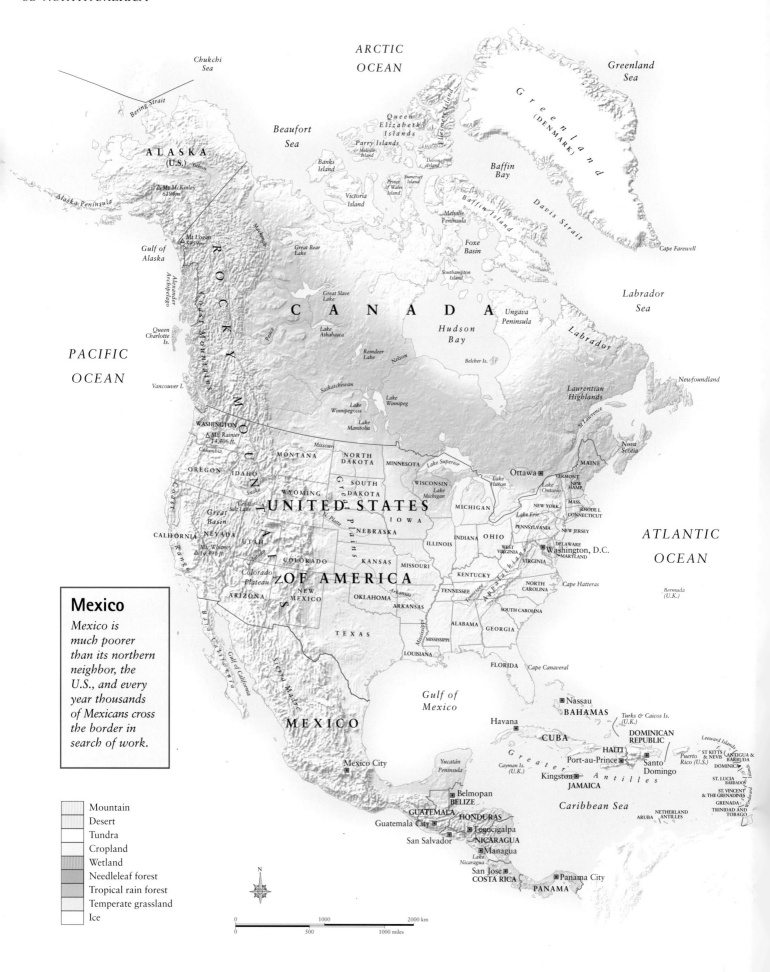

Mexico

Mexico is much poorer than its northern neighbor, the U.S., and every year thousands of Mexicans cross the border in search of work.

THE UNITED STATES OF AMERICA

Stretching across the North American continent, the United States of America is the world's leading power. A land of diverse geography and climates, it is divided into 50 states and is a "melting pot" of people and cultures. It is largely populated by descendants of immigrants who came in the past seeking a new life in the "land of opportunity."

North America was home to native populations for thousands of years before the first European explorers arrived in the 1400s. During the 1400s and 1500s, however, much of the Native Americans' land was taken over by colonies of settlers from Great Britain, France, and Spain. During the War of Independence in the 1700s, 13 colonies won freedom from British rule, and the U.S. was born. Over time the new nation expanded west until it stretched from the

Atlantic coast in the east to the Pacific coast in the west. Its vast natural resources and political stability have enabled the U.S. to become the most powerful nation in the world, exerting economic, political, and cultural influences on other countries.

The White House

The U.S. government is based in Washington, D.C. It is headed by the president, who lives in the White House.

Geographical diversity

The United States is a land of immense variety. It is the fourth largest country in the world (after Russia, Canada, and China) with an area of over 3.5 million sq. mi. (nine million sq km).

In the far north is the state of Alaska. It was bought from Russia in 1867 and became a state in 1959. Alaska borders Canada and is not connected by land to the rest of the U.S.

Although a huge state, Alaska has a tiny population of just 627,000. However, it is home to a huge array of wildlife, including bears, moose, and bald eagles. It has a dramatic landscape of glaciers and fjords and has immense natural reserves of oil and gas.

The Atlantic coast is home to some of the oldest U.S. cities such as Boston, New York City, and Philadelphia. The capital, Washington, D.C., is also located in the eastern U.S. about halfway between the north and south.

In the central northeast of the country lie the Great Lakes (Superior, Michigan, Huron, Erie, and Ontario), which occupy an area larger than most European countries.

Much of the center of the U.S. is made up of huge plains, covered with wheat fields and cattle ranches. The mighty Mississippi, Missouri, and Ohio rivers cut across the land.

Mountain high

Mount Shuksan is part of the North Cascades mountain range in the state of Washington in the northwest. It towers 7,127 ft. (2,173m) above sea level and is a popular skiing resort.

Rocky landscape

The Grand Canyon is located in the state of Arizona. This magnificent land feature has been eroded by the Colorado River over the last five million years.

Farther west, on the Great Plains, are the country's main grazing areas. This is where America's famous cowboys once herded their cattle.

The snow-capped Rocky Mountains separate the Great Plains from the arid lands and deserts of the west coast. The state of California and its major cities of San Francisco and Los Angeles lie on the west coast. Hollywood, in Los Angeles, is home to the movie industry—the hot, sunny climate has attracted moviemakers for many years. But this part of the U.S. is prone to earthquakes, and children have drills at school to practice what emergency measures to take if an earthquake strikes.

The southeast has a hot, humid climate, with areas of grassland and subtropical swampland in the state of Florida. The southeast coast is vulnerable to hurricanes in the summer. These build up over the Atlantic Ocean and batter coastal towns. Besides Everglades National Park, Florida's tourist attractions include Disney World and the John F. Kennedy Space Center at Cape Canaveral.

The U.S. also includes Hawaii, a group of volcanic tropical islands in the middle of the Pacific Ocean, over 2,294 mi. (3,700km) from the west coast of mainland U.S. Hawaii has a hot climate and is a popular tourist destination. It has been under U.S. rule since 1898, but it only became a state in 1959.

The people of the U.S.

There are 278 million people in the U.S. Most come from families whose origins are elsewhere in the world and who arrived as immigrants at some time in the last four centuries.

The original inhabitants of North America are called Native Americans. They formed hundreds of groups such as the Powhatan on the east coast, the Cherokee in the Appalachian Mountains, the Navajo in the arid lands of the southwest, and the Sioux in the Great Plains. Europeans began to settle in their lands from the early 1600s—the British in the east and the Spanish in the south and southwest. As the Europeans spread over the continent during the next 250 years many of the Native Americans died because of warfare and from exposure to new diseases. The remainder were forced to live in reservations—land set aside for them.

There are now only around two million Native Americans, living mainly in the southwest. They are proud of their ancient traditions and are determined to preserve them through folktales, festivals, art, music, and dancing.

Black Americans

During the 1600s–1800s the European settlers developed huge plantations in the southeastern U.S. to grow crops such as tobacco and cotton. They needed plenty of labor to work in the fields, so they bought slaves, who were shipped across the Atlantic from western Africa. About one million slaves in total were transported over three centuries.

Slavery was one of the main issues that divided the northern and the southern states and caused the Civil War that tore the U.S. apart between 1861 and 1865. Slavery was abolished after the war, and African-Americans became free, with the same rights as any other Americans, although racial segregation continued in the southern states. But all over the country African-Americans were still "locked" into a world of poverty and prejudice, which made it very difficult for them to prosper. In the 1950s and 1960s civil rights campaigners protested against segregation and discrimination and did a lot to increase racial equality. Today African-Americans make up 12 percent of the U.S. population.

Navajo celebration

This boy belongs to the Navajo people. He is wearing a traditional feather headdress, which is only worn for special tribal events such as powwows (gatherings with other tribes).

Sunday service

An African-American family attends Sunday service in a church in Miami, Florida.

The melting pot

During the 1800s and early 1900s huge numbers of immigrants arrived in the U.S. from Italy, Ireland, Germany, Scandinavia, and Russia. They were escaping persecution or seeking a better life. Thousands of Chinese workers were brought across the Pacific Ocean to help build the railroads, and many stayed on. Other immigrants came from Japan, the Philippines and the South Pacific Islands, Mexico, and Central and South America. Often they were trying to escape poverty and unemployment or religious and political persecution in their own countries. The U.S. was championed as the

Chinese New Year

This young Chinese-American girl has dressed up in traditional Chinese clothes to take part in a Chinese New Year parade in Los Angeles, California.

Mixed class

American schoolchildren learn about the cultures and traditions of their classmates' families. All schools in the country also proudly display the U.S. flag.

"Land of the Free," and as long as that these newcomers were loyal to the country and respected its traditions, they were generally free to create their own communities and practice their own religions.

Today the Irish community in New York City celebrates St. Patrick's Day with a big parade. New York City is also home to large Jewish and Italian communities. Chinese New Year is celebrated in the Chinatown districts of San Francisco and other large cities, and a German community in Frankenmuth, Michigan, has created a Bavarian-style town, complete with a traditional annual German beer festival. The Amish, a Protestant Christian sect originally from Switzerland, France, and Germany, have large

communities in Pennsylvania where they farm without the help of any machines. The Mormons, who follow their own form of Christianity and rules of conduct, dominate the state of Utah and its capital, Salt Lake City.

Teammates

The U.S. has a troubled history of racial segregation and discrimination, but it now has a more equal society, and children of all races play together.

Cars play a key role in American life. It was in the U.S. in 1913 that the Ford Company first started mass producing cheaper cars that ordinary people could afford, and today most families own at least one car.

In some states people can learn to drive a car at the age of 15 and drive themselves to school. But most children get to school on traditional yellow school buses. These buses are given top priority on the streets—no car can pass them when they stop to pick up or drop off children.

Part of the American dream is to make life

Building blocks
New York City, like other U.S. cities, is made up of gridlike blocks. It is famous for its skyline with towering skyscrapers such as the Empire State building.

Shopping heaven
Shopping malls, such as the Mall of America in Minneapolis, Minnesota, are located on the outskirts of towns and are full of chain stores and fast-food restaurants.

Life in the U.S.

American culture is well known throughout the world because of the international popularity of U.S. television programs and Hollywood movies. It has also influenced other countries' cultures. For example, the U.S. invented the casual look of T-shirts, jeans, sneakers, and baseball caps. They invented supermarkets and fast-food restaurants selling hot dogs, hamburgers, and pizza.

Some 77 percent of Americans live in towns and cities. Most of these are laid out in a grid pattern of neatly crisscrossing streets, forming blocks filled with buildings. The center of a city, the "downtown" area, is often a cluster of high-rise modern buildings with offices, stores, and apartment blocks. Farther out, in the suburbs, streets are lined with homes usually with large front yards and backyards. Many people go to malls to do their shopping, taking advantage of the convenience of many stores under one roof, as well as the ample parking space provided.

Off to school

Yellow school buses travel from block to block picking up and dropping off children. Most people are educated to the age of 18, when they graduate from high school.

easier, more efficient, comfortable, and enjoyable. The Americans were the first to fill their homes with electronic gadgets such as telephones, refrigerators, televisions, air-conditioning units, microwave ovens, and computers. However, prosperity has brought its own problems.

The popularity of fast and convenience foods, combined with the dependence on cars and gadgets, has had an impact on people's health. Many Americans are not eating a nutritious, balanced diet or doing enough exercise, and an estimated 18 percent of the population are obese (dangerously overweight).

American English

The Americans are united by lifestyle but also by language. Almost everyone speaks English, the country's official language. But the gradual increase in the Hispanic population (immigrants from Mexico, Central and South America, the Dominican Republic, Puerto Rico, and Cuba) makes Spanish the second most spoken language. About ten percent of the population speaks Spanish as their first language. Over 30 other languages are also spoken as first languages in the U.S.

Childhood

Like other children around the world, Americans are encouraged from early childhood to develop their talents, whether in sports, music, academics, or acting. Parents encourage their children to succeed at school and to have as much fun as possible. Special television programs are made for children, such as the internationally successful *Sesame Street*. The U.S. is also the birthplace of the theme park—Disneyland, in California, was the first, created in 1955. There are now many others, and every year they add new, more exciting, and ingenious attractions and rides.

Holidays

Christmas is the biggest public holiday in the U.S. Friends exchange Christmas cards, frequently including photographs of their families. Stores are full of decorations, and television commercials take on a seasonal note, encouraging customers to spend even more on gifts. Families gather to eat and drink and exchange gifts, and for many people in the northern U.S. Christmas is also a time of snow for tobogganing, sledding, and ice skating.

Almost as important—and more typically American—is Thanksgiving. This national holiday takes place on the last Thursday in November and marks the feast held in 1621 by the Pilgrims of the Plymouth Colony—some of the earliest European settlers in the U.S.—to celebrate the successful completion of their first year. The Thanksgiving meal traditionally consists of all-American food, such as turkey with cranberry sauce and pumpkin pie.

Another big celebration is held on July 4—Independence Day. It is a public holiday, and firework displays and concerts are held all over the country to commemorate the end of British rule and the founding of the U.S. nation.

Cartoon capers

Families flock to Disneyland in California and Disney World in Florida not only for the fun rides but to meet Disney cartoon characters such as Minnie Mouse.

Americans tend to take their vacations in the U.S. rather than traveling abroad. There are many reasons for this. One is that many Americans don't receive many "vacation days" from work, so long-distance travel is frequently impossible. Americans also have an amazing range of destinations to go to on their doorstep, from the warm beaches of Florida to the mountains and forests of the Rockies and from historic old towns like Williamsburg in Virginia to the bright lights, casinos, and fantasy hotels of Las Vegas.

Many choose to spend their vacations in the "great outdoors," taking their tents or campers to any of the numerous campgrounds. The national parks preserve the most beautiful parts of the U.S. landscape.

Some children go to summer camp during the long summer vacation period. As well as playing sports and doing arts and crafts, camps offer a wide range of activities, including computers, photography, and filmmaking.

Summer camp

Summer camp is a great place to learn new skills, have fun, and make new friends. These children are learning about the environment.

Great outdoors

The varied landscape of the U.S. is popular with campers and hikers. This family is exploring the mountains of northern California.

Sports

When they are not on vacation, Americans make full use of their precious "spare" time. Many of them participate in sports such as tennis, swimming, running, golf, soccer, volleyball, and track and field. The great national games are baseball, basketball, hockey, and football, in which players wear helmets and bulky shoulder and thigh pads to prevent injury. All of these various games are played by professionals to a high standard in national leagues. Thousands attend matches and games in huge arenas and stadiums, and millions tune in to big games on television. Every year the Superbowl often attracts the biggest television audience of the year. Baseball's leading tournament, played at the end of the season, is called the World Series.

Tackling game

Football developed from the English game of rugby. Despite its name, the foot hardly ever touches the ball. Players wear helmets and shields to protect them during tackles.

Leading sports players, such as the tennis player Jennifer Capriati and the golfer Tiger Woods, are great celebrities in the U.S., and it is the ambition of many children to achieve similar success one day. They start in school or local teams and then work their way up through state competitions to national championships.

Net gains

Tennis stars like Jennifer Capriati can earn millions of dollars competing in major Grand Slam tennis tournaments.

Many top sports players, particularly in track and field and football, also get special, intensive training at college level.

As a result of this great interest in sports and the high standards of training and of sports facilities, the U.S. is usually the leading medal winner at the Olympic Games. In fact the country has won twice as many medals as any other country since the modern games began. It has numerous outstanding champions and record beaters such as the athletes Michael Johnson, Carl Lewis, and Gail Devers.

In western states rodeos with cowboys exhibiting bull and horseback riding skills are popular sporting events. Recreational activities, such as hiking, walking, boating, hunting, and fishing, are also popular.

In the swing
Tiger Woods' success has increased the popularity of golf in the U.S. He has won most major golf championships at least once.

Entertainment capital

Surveys show that television is the most popular form of entertainment in the U.S. Some people watch it for five or six hours every day. Viewers have a choice of dozens of channels, many of them devoted to one subject such as shopping, movies, religion, or sports. The costs of making programs are met by advertising revenue, so American television programs are frequently interrupted by commercial breaks. The U.S. produces a large number of high-quality television programs, particularly sitcoms and soap operas, which are popular not only in the U.S. but all around the world.

The U.S. is also the source of most of the world's best known and most watched movies. Over 550 movies are released in the U.S. each year,

Pop power

Britney Spears is the biggest selling teenage music star. She has sold millions of records in the U.S. and throughout the rest of the world.

mostly from the main center of production in Hollywood, California, where studios have been making movies since 1911. Successful movies can make huge profits for the studios so production companies are often prepared to invest tens of millions of dollars in their most favored projects. This means they can employ the best directors, the most famous movie stars, and highly skilled technicians (cinematographers, lighting and sound engineers, and makeup artists). They also use some of the most advanced special effects techniques. Every year a glamorous awards ceremony is held in Hollywood. The Academy Awards, or Oscars, celebrate the best movies, directors, and actors of the year.

The U.S. is also an innovator in music. Many of the trends in 20th-century music came from the U.S. The blues played by African-Americans developed into jazz in the early 1900s and later into rhythm and blues (R 'n' B) and rock 'n' roll. Traditional American folksinging and country-and-western music have also had a major influence on modern pop music. Rock music is hugely popular in the U.S., and pop and rock stars

can earn millions of dollars. Rap and hip hop music developed in the black communities of U.S. cities in the 1970s and 1980s and are now part of mainstream U.S. culture.

American composers have also produced many of the most popular stage musicals such as *Kiss Me, Kate* by Cole Porter and *Oklahoma!* and *The Sound of Music* by Rodgers and Hammerstein. This worldwide influence also extends to the arts. After World War II the U.S. produced many of the major trends in painting and sculpture, from the abstract expressionism of Jackson Pollock to the pop art of Andy Warhol. The U.S. has many excellent ballet companies and orchestras that stage classical music productions.

Movie mecca

Hollywood is home to the U.S. movie industry and many movie stars. Every year it hosts the Oscars award ceremony.

Industrial giant

The U.S. has rich resources such as iron and other metals, coal, and forests. It also has plenty of oil, but as the world's greatest consumer of oil, it still has to import much of what it needs, mainly from the Middle East. The U.S. is the world's leading producer of food, and it provides almost all of its own food needs. It exports large quantities of grain, grown mainly in the plains of the Midwest. Its industries manufacture world-famous brands of sodas, breakfast cereals, clothing, cars, and aircraft.

Wheat harvest

The Midwest states are nicknamed the "bread basket" of the U.S. because of their huge fields of grains.

It also has advanced scientific industries, producing new medicines and high-tech hardware. NASA (National Aeronautics and Space Administration), the agency that was responsible for landing the first men on the Moon in 1969, remains the world's leading organization for space exploration and satellite technology.

But the cost of labor is relatively high, and many goods bought in the U.S. are

Harnessing power

Mountain rivers, such as this one in Utah, have been dammed to drive hydroelectric power plants, which help meet some of the nation's vast energy needs.

Men on the Moon

In 1969 U.S. astronauts Neil Armstrong and Buzz Aldrin became the first humans to walk on the Moon.

made abroad in countries such as China, Malaysia, and Bangladesh. In fact the U.S. has a large trade deficit—the value of its imports is far greater than the value of its exports. The U.S. is in a stronger position with its financial services, such as insurance, and its stock market, which is based in Wall Street in New York City.

About three fourths of the U.S. labor force no longer work in either industries or agriculture as they once did but instead in service industries such as finance, insurance, teaching, health care, tourism, and real estate.

Rich and poor

The U.S. ranks among the top 10 countries in the world in terms of national income per person, and the average American has more money to spend than the average citizen of just about any other country. The country has about 70 billionaires, far more than any other country. Yet many Americans are desperately poor. They live in the run-down suburbs of the cities, which are plagued by crime, violence, gang warfare, and drug abuse.

Low-income families with children, the disabled, and the elderly can get some help from the government through the welfare

Homeless

Like many cities around the world, New York City has many people who have no home and have to live on the streets, begging for food and making shelters in doorways.

system but not a great deal. Essentially in the U.S. people are expected to take care of themselves. If they become sick, they are expected to pay for their treatment, which can be very expensive. Most people take out insurance policies to cover medical care, but the poorest often cannot afford to do so, and they have to rely on one of the basic government welfare systems such as Medicare or Medicaid.

Crime and punishment

Many Americans are concerned about crime. In the U.S. over 15,000 people are murdered every year, and guns are used in at least two thirds of these murders. There have also been several news reports of shootings in schools. Gun control— the effort to control the possession of guns, thus reducing violent crime— is a major issue in the U.S. About 40 percent of the families in the country have a gun in their households. Although many own these guns for hunting purposes, some Americans argue that guns are essential for self-protection in a world where violent crime is all too common. The Bill of Rights, added to the U.S. Constitution in 1791 to protect the freedom of all American citizens, included the right to keep and bear arms—in other words, the right to possess guns and other weapons. But more and more people are calling for the number of guns on the streets to be reduced. One major cause of crime is drug abuse. This is the source of untold

Cop show

The uniform and cars of American police are familiar sights around the world because police often feature in movies and TV dramas. American police carry guns.

misery and death—not just from the drugs themselves but from the criminal activities that surround the trade in illegal drugs, which is worth billions of dollars.

The U.S. has large and tough prisons and more prisoners than any other country in the world—over 1.6 million. Many of the states have the death penalty, and convicted murderers can be executed. Prisoners condemned to die often live on the prisons'

"death row" for many years while their lawyers lodge appeals in the courts in an attempt to overturn the death sentence.

There are some success stories in the country's fight against crime. The murder rate is declining. For many years New York City had a bad reputation for crime. But recently its police force applied a policy of "zero tolerance"—they stopped anyone who was suspected of carrying out even a minor infringement such as jumping over a park fence. The strategy seems to be working, and New York City is now considered a comparatively safe city.

World power

The U.S. has been a force in world politics for over 100 years now. After World War II it led the Western world in opposing the Communist regimes of the Soviet Union and China. During the confrontation with the Soviet Union—called the "Cold War" because it never turned into a real world war—both sides built up huge arsenals of nuclear weapons. By the time the Cold War ended with the collapse of the Soviet Union and its communist system of government in 1991, each side had enough nuclear weapons to destroy the world many times over. Today the U.S. is the only superpower in the world and this has brought with it new responsibilities and concerns. The U.S. has become embroiled in conflicts that it views as a threat to world stability. In 1991 the U.S. led a coalition of countries to a war against Iraq, which had invaded neighboring Kuwait, and later in the same decade the U.S. was involved in peace-keeping efforts in Europe's troubled Balkan States.

The U.S. has a strong belief that its way of life and system of government are the best. This is based on protecting the freedom of its citizens and encouraging individuals to succeed. The nation has a powerful influence on the rest of the world through its movies, television programs, and its economic and military power. While many in the world see the U.S. way of life as desirable, others resent the influence of the U.S. They see the

Stars and stripes

The U.S. flag is called the "Stars and Stripes." It has 50 stars on it— one for each state. The red and white stripes represent the 13 original U.S. colonies.

Powerful leader

As leader of the world's only superpower the president of the United States is often called on to intervene in global conflicts. George W. Bush is the country's 43rd president.

imports of U.S. movies, language, and fast-food chains as a threat to their own countries' cultures and values.

Under threat

The political and military influence of the U.S. in the rest of the world has also earned it enemies. On September 11, 2001 an Islamic fundamentalist terrorist group called Al Qaeda hijacked planes and deliberately crashed them into the twin towers of the World Trade Center in New York City and the Pentagon in Washington, D.C. Thousands were killed in

these terrorist attacks, and the U.S. government launched a war against terrorism around the world with the backing of many other countries. The first target was Afghanistan, where the terrorists behind the September 11 attacks were believed to be hiding.

Many American people were shocked to find that there were some people who hated the U.S. so much that they were prepared to sacrifice themselves and kill so many civilians. As a result of the attacks, many Americans became more aware of their country's status as the world's superpower and the difficult responsibilities that this entails. However, the terrorist attacks also gave the American people a renewed sense of patriotism and a belief in the freedoms their nation enjoys.

CANADA

Canada is the second largest country in the world after Russia. Yet it only has a population of just over 31 million—or one person per square mile. Canada is mainly tundra (snowy, frozen wasteland) in the far north with the dramatic Rocky Mountains to the west. The central plains contain spacious prairies.

Almost all Canadians live in the southern part of the country, where temperatures are warmer—but even here the winters are long and cold, lasting from about November to April. Canada is well-prepared for the cold—the roads are quickly cleared by powerful snowplows; the houses are well-heated and insulated; people put winter tires on their cars; and they have drawers full of warm, padded winter clothes.

Canadians love winter sports such as skiing, tobogganing, and ice skating. There are major ski resorts such as Whistler in the Coast Mountains and Mont Tremblant in Quebec. But outdoor life is popular all year round, and in the summer Canadians vacation among the lakes and forests and go fishing and kayaking (canoeing).

Neighborly differences

Canada has a long border with the U.S. In fact it is the world's longest land border, and most Canadians live within 124 mi. (200km) of it. This might suggest that Canadians are similar to Americans. It is true that they have much in common—they wear similar clothes, eat similar food, shop in large out-of-town malls, watch many of the same television programs, and play hockey, baseball, and football (but to Canadian rules).

Ice match

Hockey is very popular. Protective clothing is worn to cushion falls on the hard ice.

Shifting snow

The Canadians are used to coping with the long, cold winters. This man is using a snowblower to clear snow from his driveway.

Children even go to school in the same type of yellow buses. But the Canadians are quick to point out that they are by no means the same as Americans. Their attitude to life and the world at large is different. Over half of the population has British or Irish origins, and Canada is an important member of the Commonwealth. The Queen of Great Britain, who is head of the Commonwealth, is also Canada's head of state and appears on their currency. Canada has two official languages: English and French. The country has a sizable French-speaking population, particularly in the eastern province of Quebec. French influence can be seen in architecture and food.

French influence

The large province of Quebec, stretching along the St. Lawrence River and up to the Hudson Strait, is mainly French speaking. The French were the earliest European settlers in Canada, founding the first community in 1605. They were absorbed into British Canada by conquest in 1763. The French Canadians, the Québecois, speak French with a distinctive accent, different from that spoken in France.

Each Canadian province is responsible for its own education system, and in Quebec

City life

The city of Quebec resembles a European city more than it does an American one. It is influenced by French architecture.

schoolchildren are taught in French and learn English as a second language.

Representing nearly one fourth of Canada's total population, the people of Quebec still feel that they are a distinct group within Canada, and their relationship with English-speaking Canada is sometimes strained. Many Québecois would like to see Quebec become independent from the rest of Canada. When this idea was put to voters in 1995, a slim majority voted against it, arguing that Quebec needs the rest of Canada and might not survive in isolation.

Native Americans

When the French first arrived in Canada in the early 1600s, the land was occupied by a number of Native Americans such as the Iroquois, the Algonquin, and the Cree. Some still follow their traditional way of life in the remote lands of northern Canada, fishing and trapping animals for fur. Like other Native Americans, however, many feel cheated of their ancestral lands. The Mohawks, for example, are fiercely protective of their lands near Montreal.

For many years the Canadian government tried to assimilate native peoples into the rest of society, but in 1998 the government formally apologized to the native population for the way they had been mistreated. Native groups now receive funding to help them preserve their cultures and traditions.

The Inuit have lived in the far north for many thousands of years. In 1999 the Canadian government created a new territory called Nunavut for them, covering over 780,000 sq. mi. (two million sq km).

New ways

These Cree youths learn the culture and traditions of their people but are also part of a cosmopolitan Canada—enjoying the best of both worlds.

Maple syrup and lumberjacks

The symbol of Canada is the red maple leaf, which appears on the flag. Maple trees create glorious colors in the fall, turning the Canadian landscape not just red but golden, yellow, and orange, too. In the spring a sweet, watery sap rises in the trunks of the maple trees. This can be tapped (collected) by cutting into the bark, inserting a spigot, and attaching a bucket. The sap is then boiled to evaporate much of the water and make a thick syrup. Canadians put maple syrup on pancakes and bacon at breakfast.

The forests are the source of another famous Canadian product—timber. Massive pine trees are cut down by lumberjacks (professional woodcutters) before being floated down the rivers to sawmills. Here they are turned into planks of timber or ground into pulp to make paper. Canada also has valuable mineral resources such as copper, gold, iron, and zinc, as well as oil and gas.

The Mounties

The Royal Canadian Mounted Police are nicknamed "Mounties" and are Canada's national police force. Their distinctive red uniform is worn only for special parades.

Fishing is an important industry, and many of the towns and villages of eastern Canada, in Nova Scotia and the island of Newfoundland, developed as fishing ports. Recently, however, the Canadian fishing industry has been hit by the reduction in the numbers of cod in the North Atlantic, and in 1993 the Canadian government had to ban cod fishing to allow the stocks to recover.

Most Canadians live in the big cities. The capital of Canada is Ottawa, but the largest metropolitan area (city and suburbs) is Toronto, which has a population of over 4.3 million. Montreal, a city in the province of Quebec, comes second with a population of three million.

The third largest city, Vancouver (1.8 million), is on the west coast, with views over mountains, islands, and sea inlets and a milder climate than the rest of Canada. While the rest of Canada tends to look toward the U.S. and Europe for trade, Vancouver forms part of the Pacific Rim, trading with China, Japan, and Southeast Asia.

Wood goods

Forestry is one of Canada's largest industries. It has vast forests, but environmentalists are concerned about the effects of the logging industry.

MEXICO

The Spanish-speaking country of Mexico borders the U.S. It is a hot country with deserts in the north and arid mountains in the center. In the far south there are sweltering tropical forests. Mexico is much poorer than its northern neighbor. The spending power of the average Mexican is about one fourth of that of the average American.

Ancient cultures

The great ancient civilizations of North America developed in Mexico, starting with the Olmecs in about 1200 B.C. and leading to the Maya and the Aztecs. The impressive remains of their civilizations can be seen in many parts of Mexico. They include the pyramid temples of Tenochtitlán and Chichén Itzá and the collections of sculpture, pottery, and jewelry at the

National Museum of Anthropology in the capital, Mexico City. But these civilizations collapsed with the conquest of Mexico in 1521 by the Spanish conquistador Hernán Cortés. The Spanish dominated the region until Mexico won its independence in 1836. Many of the Native Americans (or Indians as they were called because the first explorers mistakenly thought they had reached India) died from disease and maltreatment.

Today they make up one third of the population, while the rest are mestizo— a mixture of Spanish and Native American. One fourth of all Mexicans live off of the land, just as their ancient ancestors did, growing crops of beans, tomatoes, avocados, and corn, which they use to make tortilla flatbread or crisp taco shells. Mexican food is often made spicy with chili peppers called jalapeños.

The Maya

There are still Mayan villages in the Mexican rain forest. The Maya maintain many of their old customs and traditions and continue to speak Mayan languages.

City life

Most Mexicans live in the towns and cities. Mexico City, the capital, is one of the world's largest cities with a population of about 18 million. This huge number of people—many driving very old vehicles—gives Mexico City a serious pollution problem. Mexico has large reserves of oil, and it has thriving industries making steel, cars, and electrical goods. It also attracts many tourists with popular beach resorts such as Acapulco and Cancún. But wages for the majority of Mexicans are low.

Day of the Dead

Many Mexican festivals are based on their Roman Catholic faith, but some have Aztec roots. For the Day of the Dead fiesta, families go to cemeteries to light candles and offer gifts to the dead, who are thought to return to visit the living for the day. To welcome them, stores and homes are decorated with models of skeletons made of papier-mâché or dough.

Tortillas

Tortillas are thin, round patties of corn or wheat flour dough cooked on griddles. They are often served along with a meal or fried to make tacos.

Coastal resort

Tourists flock to the Pacific coast resort of Acapulco with its white-sand beaches, high-rise hotels, and hectic nightlife. Tourism is the main industry of the area.

THE CARIBBEAN

Hundreds of islands lie scattered across the Caribbean Sea. They are famous for their sandy beaches, warm, turquoise-blue seas, and easy-going lifestyle. Thirteen of these are independent countries. The largest is Cuba, which is bigger than all of the other islands put together. The smallest is St. Kitts and Nevis at just 102 sq. mi. (262 sq km).

Caribs and slaves

The Caribbean Sea is named after the Carib Indians who lived on many of the islands before the arrival of Christopher Columbus (the first European explorer) in 1492. There is still a small population of Caribs on the islands of Dominica and St. Vincent, but most of the Carib Indians were wiped out by illness and maltreatment not long after the islands were taken over and settled by European countries. Spanish, British, French, and Dutch colonizers wanted to use the islands to grow valuable crops like sugarcane. With few Carib Indians left they needed labor to work in the plantations, so they imported slaves from western Africa. The vast majority of the population in the Caribbean islands today are the descendants of these slaves.

Each island has its own story to tell and its own mix of peoples. In Cuba, for example, many of the people are descended from Spanish settlers. Some of the people living in the islands of St. Vincent and the Grenadines are descendants of Cornish fishermen from England, who settled in the region over 200 years ago.

When slavery was abolished in the 1800s, plantation owners found a new source of cheap labor in Asia and brought in workers from India and China. Today 40 percent of the population of Trinidad and Tobago are Asian.

Cuban cigars

Tobacco plants are grown in Cuba. The leaves are picked, dried, and rolled to make their world-famous cigars.

Making a living

One of the legacies of slavery is that the islands are heavily populated. They have a large number of mouths to feed, and most islands have few resources—Haiti is the poorest country of all the Americas.

Sugarcane is no longer the source of great riches. Desperate to seek more prosperous lives, many people from the Caribbean islands have left their homes and emigrated abroad. There are now large Haitian communities in the U.S. and Canada. Many thousands of people from the West Indies (as the former British islands are known) went to live in Great Britain.

The islands have had to find other means to earn incomes. Some have natural resources: Trinidad has a wealth of oil; Jamaica has bauxite (aluminum ore); and Cuba has oil, as well as nickel, copper, and chrome. Other islands grow crops for export. St. Lucia grows bananas; St. Vincent is the world's largest producer of arrowroot, a starch used as a food thickener and to make medicine and paper; Jamaica grows a high-quality coffee in its Blue Mountains; and Grenada produces spices such as cloves and nutmeg. Many islands produce rum from sugarcane.

Another way of earning income is through tourism. The Caribbean islands have all-year warmth, perfect beaches, and beautiful coral reefs for divers.

Vacation haven

Luxury resorts have been built on some Caribbean islands such as Barbados. Tourists come from all over the world.

Caribbean rhythms

In many parts of the Caribbean tourism brings little direct benefit to the people. Living on extremely low incomes, they survive by growing vegetables and fruits, such as yams, mangoes, and papayas, raising a few pigs and chickens, and fishing from small boats. People live in wooden houses with corrugated iron roofs. These roofs are vulnerable to the devastating hurricanes that sweep through the region, demolishing all in their path. Living in such conditions is hard, but the people of the

Colorful carnival

Most Caribbean countries hold annual carnivals where participants wear colorful costumes and dance through the streets to musical rhythms.

Caribbean are famous for enjoying themselves. The distinctive forms of Caribbean music reflect the history of the islands—African rhythms, Spanish guitar, and English folksinging. They have produced calypso, salsa, rumba, and soca and in Trinidad the sounds of steel bands, produced by hitting hammered oil drums. Most famous of all, perhaps, is reggae, the music of Jamaica.

Caribbeans feel that they still live in the shadows of their old European colonial rulers and the power of the U.S. to the north.

Cuba has taken a unique path of defiant independence. In 1959 the corrupt regime of President Fulgencio Batista was overthrown by a revolution led by a young lawyer, Fidel Castro. When the U.S. refused to help Castro, he looked to the Soviet Union for assistance and turned his country into a Communist state. Despite Soviet help, there was little money to go around, food was rationed, and most Cubans lived in crumbling houses, using old American cars dating from the 1950s. In 1991 the Soviet Union collapsed, and soon after Russia withdrew its support. Facing a new crisis, Castro rapidly developed a new tourist industry to attract foreign income.

Despite the poverty, Cubans enjoy one of the best health services of the region, the old are cared for, and there is little crime. The Cubans are also proud that they have created an alternative way of life, which is sociable and caring though poor. But there are doubts that it will survive when Castro is no longer there to enforce his policies.

Independent means

Reggae is closely associated with the Rastafarian movement, a religion that developed among the young people of Jamaica, focusing on their African heritage. This represents one way in which the people of the Caribbean have tried to express their unique history and identity and desire for independence. Many

Cuban rhythms

Cuban music has its origins with the African slaves who were brought to the island. Stringed instruments, such as the guitar and double bass, are very popular.

CENTRAL AMERICA

A chain of seven small countries links Mexico and North America to South America. The tapering ribbon of land called Central America separates the Atlantic Ocean from the Pacific Ocean by just 31 mi. (50km) of low-lying swampland at its narrowest point in Panama. Elsewhere the landscape rises from coasts to forests and volcanic peaks and mountains dotted with lakes.

Young helpers

Young Mayan girls have to help their mothers take care of their younger brothers and sisters. Sometimes this means missing out on going to school.

Tribal cultures

In ancient times large areas of these countries were inhabited by people ruled by or connected to the Maya. The ruins of several great Mayan temple cities are found in the north of the region such as Tikal in Guatemala and Copán in Honduras. There may be others as yet undiscovered, hidden by the dense forests of trees and undergrowth that grow rapidly in the warmth, heavy rains, and rich, tropical soil of this region.

These days many of the Native American descendants work the same soil, growing the same plants such as corn, sweet potatoes, and cocoa. They also wear clothes that reflect

their distinctive heritage. The women, for example, wear brightly colored woven jackets, shawls and headscarves. In Guatemala, Native American women wear blouses with emblems embroidered on them, showing the Mayan clan to which they belong. Nearly half the population of Guatemala is Native American, and most of the remaining half are Ladinos (a mix of Spanish and Native American).

Isolation has helped to protect the traditional ways of some Native Americans such as the Cuna people who live on the San Blas Islands off the Caribbean coast of Panama. The women wear nose rings, heavy necklaces of beads or silver coins, and embroidered armbands. They use berry juice to mark their faces with lines. On the islands the Cuna live in palm-walled huts and sleep in hammocks. They fish from small boats and come to the mainland forests to grow food in clearings.

Lakeside crops

Guatemala is the Mayan heartland of Central America. Farmers grow crops of corn, beans, squash, and tomatoes on the banks of Lake Atitlán.

European influence

The Spanish conquered Central America in the 1500s. This is why the official language of most of the countries is Spanish, although other Native American languages are spoken, many of them related to Mayan. One exception is Belize, where the official language is English because up until 1981 Belize was ruled by the British. About 20 percent of the population of Belize are Native American, while almost one third are African-Americans, the descendants of slaves.

Most of the people of Central America are Roman Catholics and attend services at churches built by the Spanish. Many are elaborate, with interiors richly encrusted with gold and statues of the saints. But local people also bring their own influence to Roman Catholicism, mixing it with ancient traditional beliefs, lighting candles and incense for their own gods, and following their ancient rituals.

Living off of the land

The main source of income for most of these countries is agriculture. Honduras, for example, grows large quantities of bananas and pineapples on huge plantations. Most of the produce is exported, particularly to the U.S. Coffee is another big export crop. Costa Rica and Nicaragua are especially famous for their coffee. A speciality of El Salvador is sweet-smelling balsam gum, a tree resin used in perfumes and ointments. Cattle are raised on ranches in the rich grasslands of Costa Rica and Panama, herded by gauchos (cowboys).

The economy of Panama is based on its famous canal. This vital shipping link was carved through the jungle to provide a passage between the Pacific and the Atlantic oceans. Before it was completed in 1914 large ships traveling between the east coast of the U.S. and the west coast had to go all the way around the southern tip of South America. The U.S. ran the Panama Canal until 2000. But it is now owned and operated by Panama, and the country earns millions of dollars from the fees paid by ships passing through it.

Panama Canal

The Panama Canal is an incredible feat of engineering. It spans 50 mi. (80km) from the Pacific to the Atlantic oceans and was completed in 1914.

Panama hats

The famous delicately woven Panama hats originated in Ecuador but were worn as protective hats by many of the workers on the Panama Canal.

Instability and opportunity

Central America has suffered from two sources of instability: nature and politics. The hills and mountains are frequently shaken by earthquakes. Added to this, hurricanes sometimes sweep through the region from the Caribbean. Belize moved its capital to Belmopan after a hurricane demolished the old capital, Belize City, in 1961. In 1998 Hurricane Mitch ripped through Honduras, Nicaragua, and Guatemala. The high winds and huge torrents of water destroyed much of Managua, the capital of Nicaragua, and tore up houses, roads, and plantations. Some 10,000 people were killed.

Such natural disasters add to the severe economic problems in these countries. The annual income across the region is about one tenth of that of the U.S. In the farmlands in the central highlands of El Salvador, for example, families live in simple thatched homes made of wattle (tree branches plastered with mud). On the flat, coastal lands of eastern Nicaragua villagers live in wooden shacks built on stilts so that they can escape the heavy rains. They use ox carts, which are better suited to the poor, muddy roads than cars or trucks.

Many people come to the cities hoping to find work but end up living in poor shantytowns.

Poverty has played its part in the violent politics of this region. In the past corrupt regimes in El Salvador, Nicaragua, and Guatemala, attempting to protect the advantages of the wealthy few, have faced armed rebellion from Communist groups. Costa Rica has escaped such troubles and has not had an army for over 50 years.

Tourism is one way in which Central American countries can boost their incomes. Costa Rica has chosen to take advantage of its magnificent tropical forests, which are home to rare species such as sloths, jaguars, and poison arrow frogs. It has declared large parts of the country to be nature reserves.

Deadly storm

Hurricane Mitch brought devastation to Central America in 1998. Relief workers cleared debris and brought food and clean water to the people affected.

Rural life

Many people in the region live in villages and have few goods and very little money. They make their livings growing crops such as wheat.

ANTIGUA AND BARBUDA

Capital
St John's
Area
170 sq. mi.
Population
66,970
Population density
395 per sq. mi.
Life expectancy
69 (m); 73 (f)
Religion
Christianity
Language
English
Adult literacy rate
90 percent
Currency
East Caribbean dollar

BAHAMAS

Capital
Nassau
Area
3,900 sq. mi.
Population
297,852
Population density
77 per sq. mi.
Life expectancy
67 (m); 74 (f)
Religion
Christianity
Languages
English, Creole
Adult literacy rate
98 percent
Currency
Bahamian dollar

BARBADOS

Capital
Bridgetown
Area
170 sq. mi.
Population
275,330
Population density
1,619 per sq. mi.
Life expectancy
70 (m); 76 (f)
Religion
Christianity
Language
English
Adult literacy rate
97 percent
Currency
Barbados dollar

Island paradise

The Caribbean island of Barbados attracts thousands of tourists every year with its tropical climate, palm trees, and sandy beaches.

BELIZE

Capital
Belmopan
Area
8,800 sq. mi.
Population
256,062
Population density
29 per sq. mi.
Life expectancy
69 (m); 74 (f)
Religion
Christianity
Languages
English, Spanish, Mayan, Garifuna
Adult literacy rate
93 percent
Currency
Belize dollar

 **CANADA**

Capital
Ottawa
Area
3,556,000 sq. mi.
Population
31,592,805
Population density
9 per sq. mi.
Life expectancy
76 (m); 83 (f)
Religion
Christianity
Languages
English, French, and other local languages
Adult literacy rate
97 percent
Currency
Canadian dollar

 COSTA RICA

Capital
San José
Area
19,500 sq. mi.
Population
3,773,057
Population density
193 per sq. mi.
Life expectancy
74 (m); 79 (f)
Religion
Christianity
Language
Spanish
Adult literacy rate
95 percent
Currency
Costa Rican colón

 CUBA

Capital
Havana
Area
42,800 sq. mi.
Population
11,184,023
Population density
262 per sq. mi.
Life expectancy
74 (m); 79 (f)
Religion
Christianity
Language
Spanish
Adult literacy rate
96 percent
Currency
Cuban peso

 DOMINICA

Capital
Roseau
Area
300 sq. mi.
Population
70,786
Population density
244 per sq. mi.
Life expectancy
71 (m); 77 (f)
Religion
Christianity
Languages
English, French patois
Adult literacy rate
90 percent
Currency
East Caribbean dollar

 DOMINICAN REPUBLIC

Capital
Santo Domingo
Area
18,700 sq. mi.
Population
8,581,477
Population density
460 per sq. mi.
Life expectancy
71 (m); 76 (f)
Religion
Christianity
Language
Spanish
Adult literacy rate
82 percent
Currency
Dominican Republic peso

EL SALVADOR

Capital
San Salvador
Area
8,000 sq. mi.
Population
6,237,662
Population density
781 per sq. mi.
Life expectancy
66 (m); 74 (f)
Religion
Christianity
Language
Spanish
Adult literacy rate
71 percent
Currency
Salvadorean colón

 GRENADA

Capital
St. George's
Area
130 sq. mi.
Population
89,227
Population density
686 per sq. mi.
Life expectancy
63 (m); 66 (f)
Religion
Christianity
Languages
English, French patois
Adult literacy rate
85 percent
Currency
East Caribbean dollar

 GUATEMALA

Capital
Guatemala City
Area
41,800 sq. mi.
Population
12,974,361
Population density
310 per sq. mi.
Life expectancy
64 (m); 69 (f)
Religion
Christianity
Languages
Spanish, Mayan
Adult literacy rate
56 percent
Currency
Quetzal

 HAITI

Capital
Port-au-Prince
Area
10,600 sq. mi.
Population
6,964,549
Population density
655 per sq. mi.
Life expectancy
47 (m); 51 (f)
Religions
Christianity, Voodoo (a blend
of Christianity and traditional
African beliefs)
Languages
French, Haitian Creole
Adult literacy rate
45 percent
Currency
Gourde

HONDURAS

Capital
Tegucigalpa
Area
43,100 sq. mi.
Population
6,406,052
Population density
148 per sq. mi.
Life expectancy
68 (m); 71 (f)
Religion
Christianity
Language
Spanish
Adult literacy rate
73 percent
Currency
Lempira

 **JAMAICA**

Capital
Kingston
Area
4,200 sq. mi.
Population
2,665,636
Population density
638 per sq. mi.
Life expectancy
73 (m); 77 (f)
Religion
Christianity
Languages
English, Jamaican patois
Adult literacy rate
85 percent
Currency
Jamaican dollar

MEXICO

Capital
Mexico City
Area
741,600 sq. mi.
Population
101,879,171
Population density
137 per sq. mi.
Life expectancy
69 (m); 75 (f)
Religion
Christianity
Languages
Spanish, Mayan dialects
Adult literacy rate
90 percent
Currency
Mexican new peso

 NICARAGUA

Capital
Managua
Area
46,400 sq. mi.
Population
4,918,393
Population density
106 per sq. mi.
Life expectancy
67 (m); 71 (f)
Religion
Christianity
Language
Spanish
Adult literacy rate
66 percent
Currency
Gold córdoba

 PANAMA

Capital
Panama City
Area
29,300 sq. mi.
Population
2,845,647
Population density
97 per sq. mi.
Life expectancy
73 (m); 79 (f)
Religion
Christianity
Languages
Spanish, English
Adult literacy rate
91 percent
Currency
Balboa

 **ST. KITTS AND NEVIS**

Capital
Basseterre
Area
104 sq. mi.
Population
38,756
Population density
373 per sq. mi.
Life expectancy
68 (m); 74 (f)
Religion
Christianity
Language
English
Adult literacy rate
97 percent
Currency
East Caribbean dollar

 ST. LUCIA

Capital
Castries
Area
240 sq. mi.
Population
158,178
Population density
659 per sq. mi.
Life expectancy
69 (m); 76 (f)
Religion
Christianity
Languages
English, French patois
Adult literacy rate
80 percent
Currency
East Caribbean dollar

 ST. VINCENT AND THE GRENADINES

Capital
Kingstown
Area
130 sq. mi.
Population
115,942
Population density
892 per sq. mi.
Life expectancy
71 (m); 74 (f)
Religion
Christianity
Languages
English, French patois
Adult literacy rate
82 percent
Currency
East Caribbean dollar

TRINIDAD AND TOBAGO

Capital
Port-of-Spain
Area
2,000 sq. mi.
Population
1,169,682
Population density
591 per sq. mi.
Life expectancy
66 (m); 71 (f)
Religions
Christianity, Hinduism
Languages
English, French, Spanish, Hindi
Adult literacy rate
98 percent
Currency
Trinidad and Tobago dollar

UNITED STATES OF AMERICA

Capital
Washington, D.C.
Area
3,535,000 sq. mi.
Population
278,058,881
Population density
79 per sq. mi.
Life expectancy
74 (m); 80 (f)
Religions
Christianity, Judaism, Islam
Languages
English, Spanish, and many native languages
Adult literacy rate
97 percent
Currency
U.S. dollar

Stars and stripes

The U.S. has a strong sense of national identity, and the flag, with its stars and stripes, is proudly displayed on national holidays.

SOUTH AMERICA

Caribbean
Sea

■ Caracas

Apure *Orinoco*

*Gulf
of Panama*

Llanos **VENEZUELA**

GUYANA

■ Georgetown

Guaviare

■ Paramaribo

Guiana
Highlands

SURINAM Cayenne ■
**French
Guiana**

ATLANTIC
OCEAN

■ Bogotá

COLOMBIA

Caquetá

Rio Negro

A M A Z O N

Marajó

Japurá

Quito ■

ECUADOR

Putumayo

Amazon

Amazon

*Gulf of
Guayaquil*

Marañón

Ucayali

Madeira

B A S I N

Iriri

Tapajós

Xingu

B R A Z I L

Jurua

S e l v a s   *Purus*

São Francisco

■ Lima

PERU

Madre de Dios

Beni

Guaporé

Teles Pires

Juruena

Araguaia

Tocantins

*Sobradinho
Reservoir*

*Mato Grosso
Plateau*

*Lake
Titicaca*

BOLIVIA

■ Brasília

*Brazilian
Highlands*

■ La Paz

Altiplano

■ Sucre

PACIFIC
OCEAN

Atacama Desert

Gran Chaco

PARAGUAY

Pilcomayo

Paraguay

■ Asunción

Salado

Paraná

Uruguay

*Mar
Chiquita*

Paraná

*Patos
Lagoon*

Aconcagua
△ 22,829 ft.

URUGUAY

*Mirim
Lake*

■ Santiago

*Juan
Fernández Is.*

■ Buenos Aires

■ Montevideo

ARGENTINA

Río de la Plata

Pampas

Colorado

Río Negro

*San Matias
Gulf*

N

Mountain
Desert
Tundra
Cropland
Wetland
Needleleaf forest
Tropical rain forest
Temperate grassland
Ice

Chiloé I.

*Los Chonos
Archipelago*

Patagonia

*San Jorge
Gulf*

ATLANTIC
OCEAN

0   500   1000 km

0   250   500 miles

Amazon

*The Amazon
Basin contains
the largest area
of tropical
forests in the
world and more
plant and animal
species than any
other habitat.*

Wellington I.

*Reina Adelaida
Archipelago*

*Bahía
Grande*

Strait of Magellan

West
Falkland

*Falkland Islands
(Islas Malvinas)
(U.K.)*

■ Stanley

East Falkland

*Tierra
Del Fuego*

Cape Horn

*South Georgia
(U.K.)*

SOUTH AMERICA

South America is a continent of immense richness and variety. In the far north Venezuela and Colombia have palm-fringed coasts on the warm Caribbean Sea. In the far south Chile and Argentina reach down to the bitterly cold island of Tierra del Fuego, just 620 mi. (1,000km) from Antarctica. Ushuaia, the capital of Argentine-controlled Tierra del Fuego, is the world's southernmost town.

The Andes form a mighty chain of soaring mountains that run up the western side of the continent. Chile, a long, thin ribbon of land, is practically all mountains and coastline. Bolivia, Peru, Ecuador, and Colombia all have extensive mountain regions. La Paz in Bolivia is the world's highest capital city at 12,005 ft. (3,660m) above sea level—so high that the air is thin from lack of oxygen, and visitors become breathless until their bodies get used to the altitude. The central west coast has stretches of hot and extremely dry desert. To the east of the Andes is the Amazon Basin, a vast region of damp, steamy tropical forest.

Life in Bolivia

A Bolivian woman carries a child on her back, wrapped snugly against the cold of the Andes Mountains.

Remnants of European rule

Like Central America, most of the South American countries are Spanish-speaking. The exception is Brazil, where the national language is Portuguese. In the past these countries were ruled as colonies by Spain and Portugal. Three small countries on the northeast coast have a slightly different history. English is spoken in Guyana, which used to be ruled by the British, and cricket is still the national sport there. Surinam was governed by the Netherlands, and the official language is Dutch. Next to Surinam is French Guiana, which is still ruled by France.

Settlers from these European countries came to live in South America, and between the 1500s and 1900s they transported hundreds of thousands of slaves from Africa to work in the plantations. The slaves were later joined by plantation workers from India, China, and Indonesia, by traders from Syria and Lebanon, and farmers and industrialists from Italy, Germany, and Scandinavia. This created the great mix of ethnic groups that is so characteristic of South America.

Church parade

*Children in a Colombian
town join a candlelit
procession in Holy Week,
the week before Easter.*

Llama farmers

*Llamas are native to South
America. They are raised
in herds for their meat and
wool, which is used to
make warm clothes.*

Native Americans

Before the Europeans came in the early 1500s South America was occupied by different groups of native South Americans, who, like the native Central Americans, later became known incorrectly as Indians. Much of the Andes was ruled as a powerful empire under the Incas of Peru—the largest native group.

These Native Americans were largely farmers who built elaborate terraces on the hillsides to grow crops of potatoes and corn and raised llamas to carry their goods along the network of high mountain paths. Other native peoples lived in ways that similarly reflected their surroundings, fishing off the coasts or growing crops in the valleys of rivers. The forest peoples of the Amazon Basin built villages in clearings and lived by gathering plants and fruits and hunting in the forest.

Floating high

This Peruvian child is in a reed boat on Lake Titicaca, which lies 12,497 ft. (3,810m) above sea level in the Andes mountains.

Poncho protection

To keep warm in the mountains Native Americans in Ecuador wear ponchos (large pieces of cloth with holes for the head).

There are still a large number of Native Americans in South America. Some live by hunting, fishing, and growing root crops in the remote tropical forests of the Amazon Basin. High in the Andes of Ecuador, Otavaleño Indians live in small, white-washed villages built of adobe mud brick. They tend sheep and grow corn and potatoes, much as their ancestors did, but today their brightly colored woven cloth is sold in the tourist market of Otavalo. These days the majority of people in South America are mestizos (mixed Spanish and Native American descent).

Bolivian piper

Bolivian music is famous for its soaring, graceful sound. It is played on instruments such as the queña (panpipes made from bamboo) and the charango (a guitar made from the shell of an armadillo).

Most South American countries are Spanish-speaking, and most highly paid professional jobs are done by people of Spanish descent living in the towns and cities.

Many Native Americans live in the country, and some people of European origin still discriminate against them. When Alejandro Toledo, a candidate of Native American ancestry, was elected president of Peru in 2001, it was considered remarkable, even though well over half of Peru's population is Native American.

Coffee and chocolate

Large areas of South America are used for farming. In the warmer regions coffee, cocoa, and sugarcane are grown on huge plantations. Grapes to make wine are grown in the cooler regions of Chile and Argentina.

Cattle are raised in the llanos (hot plains) of southern Venezuela, but the most famous cattle ranches are in the open pampas (grasslands) of Argentina and Uruguay. Here the herds are taken care of by skilled gauchos (cowboys), who ride on horseback wearing broad-rimmed hats, baggy pants, and high boots.

Gauchos eat *asado* (beef barbecued on a spit by an open fire). They drink a type of tea called yerba maté.

Sun beans

After harvesting, coffee beans are spread on cement floors or tables to dry in the sun. They are turned regularly for seven to 15 days.

Horse skills

Horseback riding skills are highly valued in South America, and many children learn to ride at a young age. This boy is showing his skills at a festival in Chile.

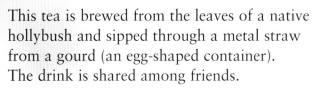

This tea is brewed from the leaves of a native hollybush and sipped through a metal straw from a gourd (an egg-shaped container). The drink is shared among friends.

Food differs from country to country, but a typical meal across the region consists of a piece of fried beef or chicken, eaten with rice or boiled potatoes and salad, and served with fried plantains, a banana-like vegetable. Tasty snacks include charcoal-grilled corn and empanadas (spicy, savory pastries).

It is hard to make a living by farming in many regions in South America. This is why some farmers, especially in Colombia, have turned to growing crops that are used to make illegal drugs such as cocaine and marijuana. The drug trade, run by armed criminal gangs, causes terror and instability in the region. Exported largely to the U.S., the drug crops earn the farmers large sums of money. South American governments struggle to persuade the farmers to grow alternative crops. The farmers are worried they will not earn enough to feed their families.

Shantytowns

The majority of South Americans live in towns and cities. Most of these were founded by European settlers from the 1500s onward, but their old historic centers, with their grand palaces and their richly decorated Roman Catholic churches, are now surrounded by modern high-rise buildings and streets busy with traffic.

Poor families come to the cities from the country in the hope of finding work. But work is not always easy to find, and many of them end up living in shacks in the shantytowns on the outskirts of the cities, without running water, proper drainage, or legal electricity supplies. Furthermore the shantytowns are often built on poor, steep land and can be washed away in heavy storms.

Many of the poorest children from the shantytowns cannot afford to go to school because they have to earn money for food—although education is usually free up to the age of 14. Some do not have homes but sleep on the streets, sheltering in cardboard boxes. These "street children" may eke out a living by doing odd jobs, begging, or stealing.

Poverty is a problem that faces most countries in South America. Many are rich in resources—Venezuela, Ecuador, and Argentina have oil; Brazil has gold and iron ore; Chile has copper; Colombia has coal and emeralds; Bolivia has tin and natural gas; and Guyana and Brazil have bauxite (aluminum ore).

They also have plenty of fertile land. However, their economies are not strong enough to guarantee long-term wealth for their

Soccer fans

South American national soccer teams often compete against teams from around the world in international contests. Millions of fans watch the games on television.

Fetching water

Most shantytowns do not have clean water supplies, and people have to buy containers of water. Cholera, a disease caused by dirty water, is a problem in many South American countries.

governments, but economic difficulties have continued to cause instability. In early 2002 Argentina's huge debts to foreign banks made the country virtually bankrupt.

Culture and sports

The colorful, varied, and complex world of South America has been captured by some of its best-known writers such as Jorge Luis Borges of Argentina and Gabriel García Márquez of Colombia. It is also reflected in the music, from the rhythmic folk songs played with guitars, accordions, tambourines, and the Andean panpipes to the passionate, up-tempo music of the tango, the fiery dance of Argentina.

The most popular sport in South America is soccer. Children practice their soccer skills from an early age, hoping one day to become professional soccer players. The great star of Argentinian soccer of the 1980s, Diego Maradona, was brought up in a shantytown in the capital, Buenos Aires. His foot-juggling tricks helped him become a professional soccer player at the age of just 15.

In Bogotá, the capital of Colombia, street children play a more dangerous game, clinging onto the bumpers of moving buses and "surfing" on flattened wooden fruit crates.

people. As a result, they have suffered from unstable governments. Most countries have been taken over by military dictators in the past, and some of these have been particularly cruel. When Argentina was under military rule in the 1970s, at least 30,000 young people "disappeared." In a ruthless effort to stamp out left-wing terrorism they were murdered by government agents or died in prison. Since the 1980s all of the military dictators have been replaced by democratic

Gold mining

Brazil, Peru, and Venezuela are among the South American countries with gold supplies. Thousands of miners dig the ground searching for gold deposits.

BRAZIL

Brazil is by far the largest country in South America. Its main language is Portuguese, not Spanish—Brazil was a Portuguese colony for over 300 years until 1822. The north of the country is home to the densely forested Amazon Basin. The city of Rio de Janeiro lies on the coast and is famous for its colorful carnivals.

All the world

When Brazil became a Portuguese colony in 1500, it was already populated by about two million Native Americans. Many of them were killed in war or by diseases or pushed back into the forests. The Portuguese established plantations to grow sugarcane, coffee, cocoa, and cotton, and they brought about four million west African slaves to the country to work on these plantations.

The European settlers stayed mainly around the coasts, where they were joined by people from all over the world. These early settlers have created a country with a huge mix of peoples and cultures. The greatest showpiece of Brazil's vibrant energy is its famous carnival week in Rio de Janeiro. Performers dressed in amazing, colorful costumes parade through the streets dancing to the samba—a heady blend of European music and African rhythms.

Natural wealth

Brazil has rich resources. The mines produce gold, iron ore, and bauxite (aluminum ore). There is also oil and natural gas. Brazil is South America's leading industrial nation, and its factories produce cars, airplanes, textiles, and processed foods. It is also the world's largest producer of sugar and coffee.

Rio de Janeiro

Rio de Janeiro lies among rain forest-clad cliffs on the Atlantic coast. Its beautiful scenery and beaches make it a popular tourist destination.

Colorful carnival

Work on the lavish carnival costumes begins months before the event. The date varies from year to year, but it is usually held during the peak of summer.

The Amazon River is the most important geographical feature of Brazil. It is the world's second longest river after the Nile and has a network of rivers leading from it to form the Amazon Basin. Much of the Amazon Basin is swampland and forest—it is the world's largest tropical rain forest. Roads have been built through the forest to open up the region for development. Loggers cut down the trees for timber, and international companies mine for gold and bauxite. Farmers use the cleared land to grow crops and raise cattle. As a result, large areas of forest have been destroyed.

The Amazon rain forest is home to Native Americans who follow patterns of life that have changed very little for thousands of years. They hunt with poison arrows, live in round, thatched homes, and use forest plants as medicine. But many of the forest's peoples have seen their lives change dramatically as industries and new settlers invade their land.

The Brazilian government has to make difficult choices. On the one hand, it wants to preserve the forest and the people who live there. On the other, it wants its people to prosper by exploiting the country's resources. As a symbol of its desire to modernize, in 1961 Brazil created an entirely new capital, called Brasília, closer to the center of the country than the old capital, Rio de Janeiro.

ARGENTINA

Capital
Buenos Aires
Area
1,055,400 sq. mi.
Population
37,384,816
Population density
35 per sq. mi.
Life expectancy
72 (m); 79 (f)
Religion
Christianity
Languages
Spanish, English, Italian
Adult literacy rate
96 percent
Currency
Argentine peso

 BOLIVIA

Capital
La Paz (administrative);
Sucre (judicial)
Area
418,200 sq. mi.
Population
8,300,463
Population density
20 per sq. mi.
Life expectancy
62 (m); 67 (f)
Religion
Christianity
Languages
Spanish, Quechua, Aymara
Adult literacy rate
83 percent
Currency
Boliviano

 BRAZIL

Capital
Brasília
Area
3,261,200 sq. mi.
Population
174,468,575
Population density
53 per sq. mi.
Life expectancy
59 (m); 68 (f)
Religion
Christianity
Languages
Portuguese, Spanish, English,
French
Adult literacy rate
85 percent
Currency
Real

 CHILE

Capital
Santiago
Area
288,800 sq. mi.
Population
15,328,467
Population density
53 per sq. mi.
Life expectancy
73 (m); 79 (f)
Religion
Christianity
Language
Spanish
Adult literacy rate
95 percent
Currency
Chilean peso

 COLOMBIA

Capital
Bogotá
Area
400,600 sq. mi.
Population
40,349,388
Population density
101 per sq. mi.
Life expectancy
67 (m); 75 (f)
Religion
Christianity
Language
Spanish
Adult literacy rate
91 percent
Currency
Colombian peso

 ECUADOR

Capital
Quito
Area
106,800 sq. mi.
Population
13,183,978
Population density
123 per sq. mi.
Life expectancy
69 (m); 74 (f)
Religion
Christianity
Languages
Spanish, Quechua, and
local languages
Adult literacy rate
90 percent
Currency
U.S. dollar and sucre

Learning to hunt

These children live in the Amazon Basin in Brazil. They are learning how to use a bow and arrow so that they can hunt for food.

GUYANA

Capital
Georgetown
Area
75,900 sq.mi.
Population
697,181
Population density
9 per sq. mi.
Life expectancy
62 (m); 68 (f)
Religions
Christianity, Hinduism, Islam
Languages
English, Hindi, Urdu, and
local dialects
Adult literacy rate
98 percent
Currency
Guyanese dollar

 PARAGUAY

Capital
Asunción
Area
153,200 sq. mi.
Population
5,734,139
Population density
37 per sq. mi.
Life expectancy
71 (m); 77 (f)
Religion
Christianity
Languages
Spanish, Guarani
Adult literacy rate
92 percent
Currency
Guarani

 PERU

Capital
Lima
Area
493,600 sq. mi.
Population
27,483,864
Population density
56 per sq. mi.
Life expectancy
68 (m); 73 (f)
Religion
Christianity
Languages
Spanish, Quechua, Aymara
Adult literacy rate
89 percent
Currency
New sol

 **SURINAME**

Capital
Paramaribo
Area
62,300 sq. mi.
Population
433,998
Population density
7 per sq. mi.
Life expectancy
69 (m); 74 (f)
Religions
Christianity, Hinduism, Islam
Languages
Dutch, Sranang Tongo,
English, Hindustani
Adult literacy rate
93 percent
Currency
Suriname guilder

 URUGUAY

Capital
Montevideo
Area
67,700 sq. mi.
Population
3,360,105
Population density
50 per sq. mi.
Life expectancy
72 (m); 79 (f)
Religion
Christianity
Language
Spanish
Adult literacy rate
97 percent
Currency
Uruguayan peso

 VENEZUELA

Capital
Caracas
Area
340,200 sq. mi.
Population
23,916,810
Population density
67 per sq. mi.
Life expectancy
70 (m); 77 (f)
Religion
Christianity
Language
Spanish
Adult literacy rate
91 percent
Currency
Bolívar

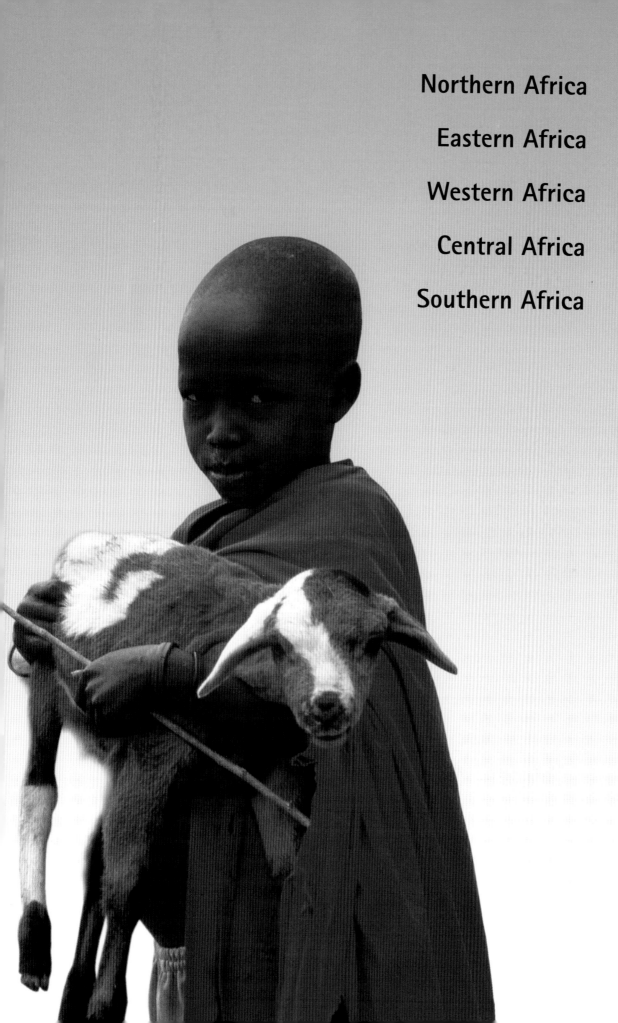

Northern Africa

Eastern Africa

Western Africa

Central Africa

Southern Africa

AFRICA

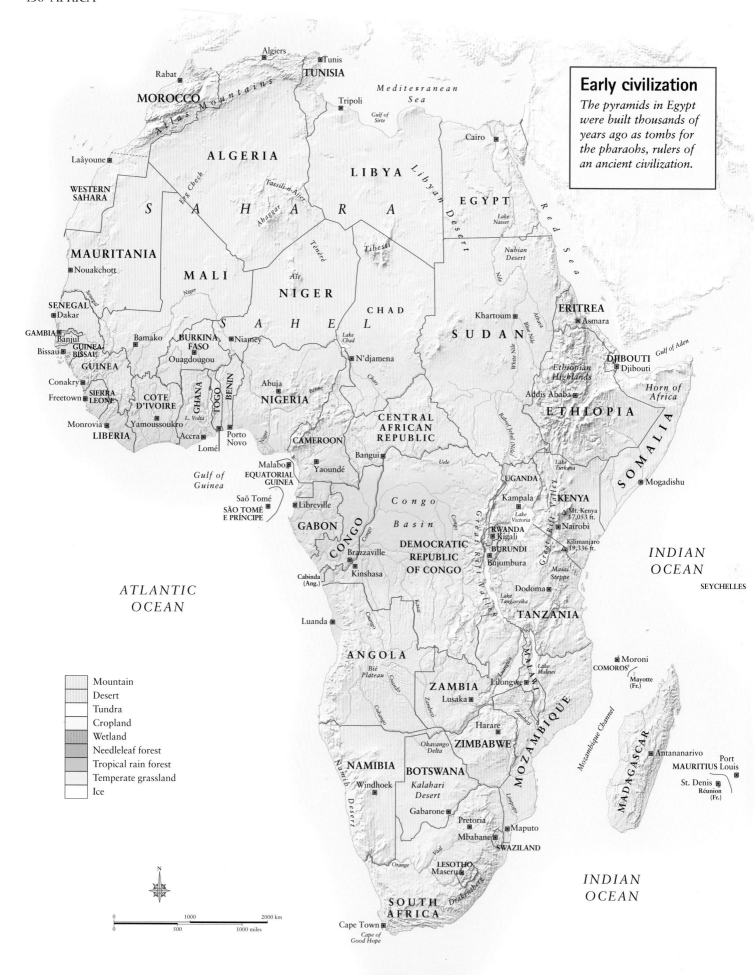

Algiers
Tunis
TUNISIA
Rabat
MOROCCO
Tripoli
Mediterranean Sea
Gulf of Sirte
Cairo
Atlas Mountains

Laâyoune
ALGERIA
LIBYA
EGYPT
Libyan Desert
Lake Nasser
Red Sea

WESTERN SAHARA
S A H A R A
Erg Chech
Tassili-n-Ajjer
Ahaggar
Tibesti
Ténéré
Nubian Desert
Nile

Early civilization

The pyramids in Egypt were built thousands of years ago as tombs for the pharaohs, rulers of an ancient civilization.

MAURITANIA
Nouakchott
MALI
Air
NIGER
S A H E L
CHAD
SUDAN
Khartoum
ERITREA
Asmara
Blue Nile
Atbara
Gulf of Aden

SENEGAL
Dakar
Senegal
Niger
Bamako
BURKINA FASO
Ouagadougou
Niamey
Lake Chad
N'djamena
Chari
DJIBOUTI
Djibouti
White Nile

GAMBIA
Banjul
GUINEA BISSAU
Bissau
GUINEA
Conakry
Freetown
SIERRA LEONE
COTE D'IVOIRE
GHANA
L. Volta
TOGO
BENIN
Abuja
NIGERIA
Benue
Addis Ababa
Ethiopian Highlands
Horn of Africa
ETHIOPIA

Monrovia
LIBERIA
Yamoussoukro
Accra
Lomé
Porto Novo
CAMEROON
CENTRAL AFRICAN REPUBLIC
Bangui
Uele
Bahr el Jebel (Nile)
Malabo
EQUATORIAL GUINEA
Yaoundé
Lake Turkana
SOMALIA

Gulf of Guinea
São Tomé
SÃO TOMÉ E PRÍNCIPE
Libreville
GABON
Congo
Congo Basin
UGANDA
Kampala
Lake Victoria
KENYA
△ Mt. Kenya 17,053 ft.
Nairobi
Mogadishu

CONGO
Congo
Brazzaville
DEMOCRATIC REPUBLIC OF CONGO
Kinshasa
RWANDA
Kigali
BURUNDI
Bujumbura
△ Kilimanjaro 19,336 ft.
Masai Steppe
INDIAN OCEAN

ATLANTIC OCEAN
Cabinda (Ang.)
Kasai
Great Rift Valley
Dodoma
Lake Tanganyika
TANZANIA
SEYCHELLES

Luanda
Cuango
Kasai
ANGOLA
Bié Plateau
Cuando
Zambezi
ZAMBIA
Lusaka
Luangwa
Lake Malawi
MALAWI
Lilongwe
Moroni
COMOROS
Mayotte (Fr.)

Mountain	
Desert	
Tundra	
Cropland	
Wetland	
Needleleaf forest	
Tropical rain forest	
Temperate grassland	
Ice	

Cubango
Okavango Delta
Harare
ZIMBABWE
Zambezi
MOZAMBIQUE
Mozambique Channel
MADAGASCAR
Antananarivo
Port Louis
MAURITIUS

NAMIBIA
Windhoek
Kalahari Desert
BOTSWANA
Gabarone
Limpopo
Pretoria
Maputo
Mbabane
SWAZILAND
St. Denis
Réunion (Fr.)

Namib Desert
Orange
Vaal
LESOTHO
Maseru
Drakensberg

N

0	1000	2000 km
0	500	
	1000 miles	

Cape Town
SOUTH AFRICA
Cape of Good Hope
INDIAN OCEAN

NORTHERN AFRICA

Across northern Africa stretches a string of countries—Morocco, Algeria, Tunisia, Libya, and Egypt. The coasts of all five line the Mediterranean Sea. Behind these coasts lies the world's largest desert, the Sahara—a vast expanse of sand dunes, rock, and gravel that bakes beneath the cloudless skies. Al Aziziyah in Libya holds the record for the world's highest temperature: 136.4°F (58°C) in the shade.

The main cities and towns in northern Africa lie near the Mediterranean coast or, in the case of Egypt, along the mighty Nile River. The coastal areas are not as hot and arid as the desert land in the south, and there is more fertile land for growing crops.

Morocco and Algeria were once French colonies, and the French influence can be seen in the architecture of their capitals, Rabat and Algiers. However, the majority of people in northern Africa are Arabs. Their descendants conquered the region in the 900s, bringing with them the Islamic faith.

Mountain life

In the south of Morocco lie the Atlas Mountains. The climate is cooler in this area so children wear warmer clothes.

Plant life

The sand dunes and rocky wastelands of the Sahara deter most plants from growing, but dotted across the vast, empty desert are green oases. Each oasis has a well at its center that taps underground reserves of freshwater. Date palms grow around the wells, sometimes in the thousands. They provide valuable shade in which vegetables can be grown. Rain falls in coastal regions and in the Atlas Mountains, which cross Morocco and Algeria. Here farmers grow oranges, lemons, grapes, and beans.

Water supplies

Northern Africa has few rivers, but it has one very famous one. The Nile River snakes through Egypt to the Mediterranean Sea—a journey of 14,135 mi. (6,670km). Farmers draw water from the river to irrigate their crops. From the air the Nile Valley looks like a green ribbon. On either side of it lies the baking desert. But underneath the desert are huge supplies of water that collected on top of layers of impermeable rock in ancient times. This water is pumped to the surface and carried across the desert by huge pipelines. In Libya the Kufra Basin, a single underground water reserve, contains more water than the Nile produces in 220 years.

Peoples of the Nile Valley

The Nile River gave rise to one of the world's earliest civilizations in ancient Egypt more than 5,000 years ago. But it was the Romans who brought the countries of northern Africa together, gradually conquering the entire Mediterranean coast from 146 B.C.

During A.D. 600 the Arabs swept across the region, bringing with them the religion of Islam. Almost all of the people of these lands are now Muslim, and the main language is Arabic. French is also spoken in Morocco, Tunisia, and Algeria, as these countries were governed by France until the 1950s and 1960s.

Nomadic herders

The Tuareg people are nomadic Berbers who live by herding camels and goats in the desert regions of southern Algeria and Libya. Their traditional dress is made of long strips of black or blue cotton.

Everyday life

Most people in northern Africa live by farming, sea-fishing, trade, or craftwork. Others work in the tourist industry, taking care of the thousands of foreign visitors who come to enjoy the winter sun on the beaches of Morocco and Tunisia or to visit the sights of ancient Egypt.

In the traditional villages people live in flat-roofed houses made with mud bricks and palm timbers. Most of the big cities are close to the coast with busy streets crammed with cars and buses. Tall, modern buildings have been built around the old quarters with their winding streets and souks (covered markets). The souks are packed with hundreds of tiny stalls selling fruit, spices, handwoven rugs, baskets, and jewelry.

Five times a day the loudspeakers in the city mosques resonate with the voices of the muezzins (religious leaders) calling Muslims to prayer. When worshipers enter a mosque, they remove their shoes and wash in the fountains before praying in the cool, shaded halls. In Morocco mosques are adorned with pottery tiles, which are attached to the walls in elaborate patterns—an art form called *zellij*.

Head start

This young acrobat is one of many entertainers who perform in the central square of Marrakech, Morocco. Jugglers, magicians, snake charmers, and storytellers also compete to catch the eyes of shoppers and passersby.

Political troubles

All of the countries of northern Africa are led by presidents, except Morocco, which has a king (Mohammed VI, who succeeded to the throne in 1999). Since gaining independence from France in 1956 Tunisia has been ruled by one political party. When elections were held in 1999, the country's president, Zine El Abidine Ben Ali, won with 99 percent of the vote, and other countries were suspicious about whether this result was made up.

Libya is ruled as a strict Islamic state by a military government under Colonel Mu'ammar Muhammad al-Gadhafi, who came to power in 1969. Economic sanctions were imposed on Libya by the United Nations during the 1990s because the country refused to hand over suspected terrorists to an international court for a trial. The sanctions were lifted in 1999, and Libya has been developing new trade links.

Neighboring Algeria has been a troubled country since 1991. Conflict between the ruling regime and Islamic fundamentalists has cost more than 75,000 lives. The country has the world's fourth largest reserves of natural gas and major deposits of oil. But the political turmoil has weakened the economy, and there is high unemployment.

The difficulties of life at home have caused many people from northern Africa to seek new lives abroad, especially in France, Spain, and Belgium and in the Middle East.

The pyramids

The ancient Egyptians built the pyramids at Giza about 4,500 years ago as tombs for their kings. Today they attract thousands of tourists.

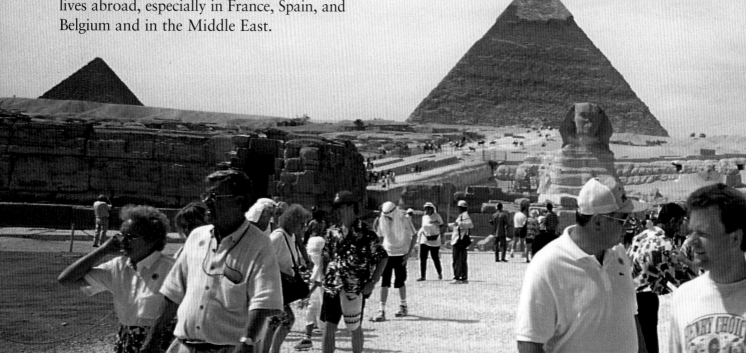

Entertainment

Festivals in northern Africa are big, colorful events. In Egypt *moulids* (giant fairs and religious celebrations all rolled into one) are held to celebrate the birthdays of local saints or holy people. In Morocco people travel a long way to take part in the annual Berber *moussems* (bride fairs) in the Atlas Mountains. At the bride fairs Berber men and women can look for marriage partners.

Television is an increasingly popular form of entertainment, and sports such as soccer are played throughout the region.

Festival time

At the annual Fantasia Festival in Morocco villagers participate by riding their horses and firing their guns.

Soccer star

The Algerian-born soccer player Zinedine Zidane was a key player in the victorious French World Cup team in 1998 and is a popular hero in Algeria.

EASTERN AFRICA

Tthe grasslands of Kenya and Tanzania, with their herds of zebras and wildebeest, are some of the best-known landscapes of eastern Africa. So too are the white-sand beaches and palm trees of the Seychelles. The drier landscapes of Sudan, parts of Ethiopia, Eritrea, and Somalia are tough places to live, frequently suffering droughts and famine.

Say it with beads

Masai women wear elaborate disks of beads. The number and colors of the beads show whether a woman is married and how many children she has. They also show her wealth.

The Masai

Some 300,000 Masai people live in Kenya and Tanzania, and many follow the traditional way of life, herding cattle in the grasslands. A Masai man's wealth is measured by the size of his cattle herd. Small family groups live in kraals (encampments). A hedge of thornbush surrounds their houses, which are made of mud, dung, and tree branches. Their main foods are meat, milk, and fresh blood, drawn from living cattle and mixed with powdered berries.

Living by the seasons

The Nuer and Dinka peoples live along the banks of the Nile River in southern Sudan, raising cattle, growing millet, and fishing. When the Nile floods in the rainy season, they move from the riverside to villages on higher land. In the drier north of Sudan and in Somalia some people live as nomadic herders, while other more settled villagers cluster around oases.

In Ethiopia the land ranges between desert and the high plateaus, where most Ethiopians live. Here there is enough rainfall to graze cattle and grow crops such as wheat, beans, and coffee.

Deadly aim

Masai men, in their traditional red cloaks, take pride in their skills and courage as warriors. These same skills are also needed to protect their herds as they roam the grasslands.

Foreign influences

Ethiopia was the first country in Africa to adopt Christianity, in the early A.D. 300s. Islam spread south from northern Africa after the A.D. 300s and was also brought to the coasts of eastern Africa by Arab traders from Yemen and Oman. The white-stone towns on the islands of Zanzibar in Tanzania and Lamu in Kenya still have a noticeable Arab influence.

In the 1800s and 1900s Europeans took over much of eastern Africa as colonies. As well as exerting a cultural and political influence, the European colonizers turned much of the fertile land into large farms to produce crops for export. By the 1960s the African nations had gained their independence.

Health education

A movie is being made with puppets to teach people about malaria, a common disease in eastern Africa. It is caused by a germ carried by mosquitoes, which spread the disease by biting people.

The Arab dhow

This traditional sailing boat was used by Arab traders along the coast of eastern Africa 4,000 years ago. Today dhows are used for coastal trade and as fishing boats.

Tourism

The grasslands, or savannas, of eastern Africa are home to a rich variety of wildlife such as cheetahs, lions, and zebras. Large areas have been set aside as national parks and game reserves, where animals are protected. Every year many tourists visit Kenya and Tanzania to go on safaris. Park rangers take them into the reserves in all terrain vehicles, and they are able to watch the animals at close quarters. Tourism brings in much needed foreign income and provides jobs.

Tourists also visit the coast to enjoy the warm sea and sand. The Seychelles, a set of 115 islands off the coast of Kenya, are famous for their white-sand beaches. These islands do not have much to export to the rest of the world except fish, coconut products, and cinnamon. Three fourths of their income comes from tourism.

Champion runner

Ethiopia's Derartu Tulu was first across the finishing line in the 10,000m final at the Sydney Olympics in 2000.

Record breakers

Eastern Africa has produced some fine athletes. The Ethiopian Miruts Yifter won both the 5,000m and the 10,000m races at the 1980 Olympics in Moscow. Ethiopian runner Belayneh Dinsano held the world record for the men's marathon for ten years after breaking the record in the Netherlands in 1988. The new Ethiopian hero is the 10,000m world record holder, Haile Gebrselassie.

Kenya came to world attention at the 1968 Olympics in Mexico City, when Kip Keino won the 1,500m and Naftali Temu won the 10,000m race. In 1998 Kenya's Paul Tergat broke the record for the men's half-marathon in Milan, and in 1999 Tegla Loroupe broke the record for the women's marathon in Berlin.

WESTERN AFRICA

The Sahara Desert extends right across Africa. Along its southern border it gradually becomes less dry, forming a broad band of semidesert known as the Sahel. Farther south toward the equator and toward the coasts there is more rainfall, and the landscape becomes greener. The Niger River flows across western Africa from Sierra Leone to Nigeria, passing through the dry landscapes of Mali on the way.

Desert dwellers

Some countries in western Africa, such as Mali, Mauritania, and Niger, are mainly desert and semidesert. Here nomadic people, such as the Tuareg of northern Niger, live by herding, traveling with their camels, goats, and flocks of sheep in search of fields. The children attend school on the move in "tent schools."

Other desert dwellers have settled around oases, where they live in mud-brick homes and grow dates, vegetables, and grains. Life for many people is becoming harder as the Sahel gets drier and the population grows. Niger has one of the fastest growing populations in the world. Nearly half of its people are under the age of 15.

Mud-brick mosques

These mosques in Djenné, Mali, are made of mud. Here Muslim culture comes together with African building materials.

Village life

Closer to the coasts and the equator the landscape changes to grassland and forests. The people here live in villages in round mud houses with roofs made of palm thatch. The women look after the household and grow corn, peanuts, yams, and cassava to feed the family. The men tend herds of cattle and goats.

Much of the southern coast is lined with mangrove swamps and islands. Many people in southern Togo and Benin live in fishing villages raised above the water on stilts.

Slavery

From the 1500s to the 1800s millions of African slaves were bought by Europeans and sent to work on sugar plantations in the Caribbean and South America. They were also taken to North America to work on tobacco and cotton plantations.

Whole familes and villages were shipped to the Americas as slaves. They were treated very cruelly. Shackled in chains, they were crammed onto slave ships for the long journey across the Atlantic Ocean. Two thirds of the slaves died during the voyage or from disease, ill treatment, and overwork when they reached the plantations.

By the time the slave trade ended in the 1800s, 12 million Africans had been shipped through slave ports such as the Isle de Gorée in Senegal.

Fish eaters
This Mauritanian girl is taking home fish for the family's meal. Fish is an important food on the west African coast. The Senegalese are some of the biggest fish eaters in the world—second only to Japan.

Soccer crazy
Soccer is played in towns and villages throughout western Africa, although there are few true grass fields.

Traditional ways

As in most parts of Africa the people use a mixture of traditional and Western medicine. Many Western medicines are too expensive, and life-threatening diseases, such as malaria and tuberculosis, are widespread. Traditional healers, or witch doctors, are honored—and sometimes feared—members of the community. The neem tree has been used by witch doctors for hundreds of years for its remarkable medicinal powers and is now being tested by international pharmaceutical companies.

The old tribal religions based on ancestor worship are still practiced alongside Islam and Christianity. In the traditional masquerade, performers disguised from head to foot in robes and elaborate masks dance and act out stories about the spirits and ancestors.

Funeral dance
A funeral is an occasion for traditional ceremonies and dancing. These masked Dogon dancers are performing at a funeral in Mali.

Most people remain loyal to their tribes and speak a local language such as Hausa and Ibo in Nigeria and Mossi in Burkina Faso. Many tribes are still ruled by powerful chiefs. The Asante of Ghana, for example, have the Asantehene as their chief. He attends ceremonies wearing spectacular robes and a gold crown and sits on a gold throne. In Mali the chiefs have griots (their own musical entertainers), who write songs about tribal history. Traditional musicians in western Africa play a *kora*, which looks like a lute or guitar and sounds like a harp.

City life

The larger cities of western Africa have modern high-rise office blocks and shopping malls. Wealthy people enjoy comfortable lives, with air-conditioned homes, satellite television, computers, and high-tech audio equipment. Their children often go on to higher education, and many study abroad.

But for the vast majority of people, life is not like that at all. They live in the sprawling suburbs in small apartments or shacks, often without running water or electricity. Most children go to elementary schools, which are free, but many receive little further education because their parents are too poor to pay the tuition.

Street vendor
In the cities some people eke out a living by selling cigarettes, matches, shoelaces, or like this boy, toothpaste.

Arts and crafts

Western Africa has a proud arts and crafts tradition. The craftsmen of the old kingdom of Benin were famous for their bronze casting, and this skill is used today to make copperware and brass. An even more ancient skill was carving ivory. However, now that it is illegal to kill elephants for their ivory tusks craftsmen use wood for their intricately carved boxes and sculptures.

In the past jewelry and masks were designed for traditional ceremonies, but today they are more likely to be sold to tourists. Craft goods made for the tourist markets range from elaborate traditional baskets to toy models of motorbikes made of bent wire.

A particularly popular product is the articulated chair, a low, thronelike portable chair made of two pieces of carved wood that slot together ingeniously.

West African painting is colorful and lively and often depicts daily life in a humorous way.

Political troubles

In recent years Sierra Leone and Liberia have been torn apart by vicious civil wars. As a result of these troubles, Sierra Leone has one of the lowest life expectancies in the world. The average life expectancy is just 36 years for men and 39 years for women.

Most countries in western Africa are ruled as republics. The president and government are elected by the people, but the elections are not always free and fair. Ethnic loyalties are also important and often the cause of conflict.

In recent years the Nigerian army has stepped in to take over power in their country. Many countries in western Africa, including Ghana, Côte d'Ivoire, Burkina Faso, Mauritania, and Gambia, have also had military governments.

But there are signs of change in some countries. After many years of military rule Ghana had free elections in the 1990s and now has a multiparty democracy.

Giant puppets

In Mali masked dancers take part in a ritual performed by most of the village in June before the arrival of the rains. This colorful giant puppet conceals several performers.

CENTRAL AFRICA

Much of central Africa lies on the equator, where it is hot and there is plenty of rain. With the exception of Chad, which spreads across the semidesert of the Sahel into the Sahara, the land is covered with rain forests or grasslands. The Democratic Republic of Congo is crossed by rivers and dotted with lakes. The east side rises up to mountains and the small countries of Rwanda and Burundi.

Pygmies

The Mbuti pygmies live in the rain forests of the Democratic Republic of Congo. The men hunt for wild animals using poisoned arrows. The women collect roots, berries, and wild plants. The average height of the men is 4 ft. 3 in. (134cm), and the women average 4 ft. (124cm).

Self-sufficiency

These pygmy children are enjoying a meal that they have just prepared. The children learn at a very early age how to construct their own conical huts and how to build fires.

Natural resources

In the north of Chad nomads shepherd their sheep and goats across the parched land in search of grazing areas. In the more fertile south and in the Central African Republic nonnomadic farmers grow corn, peppers, tomatoes, okra, and cassava.

Cattle are raised in the region's grasslands, and smoked beef is a very popular dish in these areas. Caterpillars are also eaten throughout central Africa as a delicacy.

Many countries in central Africa are rich in natural resources, including diamonds, copper, iron, bauxite, manganese, uranium, and timber. In addition to minerals, Gabon has oil supplies, which has made it one of the richest countries in Africa.

Gabon's wealth has helped it maintain a stable government. While it is a multiparty democracy, poorer countries in the region have suffered from political unrest.

Independence and turmoil

In the late 1800s Europeans took large areas of central Africa as colonies. They helped themselves to raw materials, such as timber and copper, to use in industries back at home and forced Africans to work on their plantations.

In the 1960s and 1970s all the countries of central Africa won their independence. This often happened quickly, leaving weak systems of government that could be taken over by tyrants.

The Central African Republic was ruled by Jean Bedel Bokassa from 1966 to 1979. He proclaimed himself emperor and had a golden throne decorated with an eagle. He spent a large fortune on himself and on his grand coronation. Bokassa was overthrown after his imperial guard massacred 100 schoolchildren who protested against being forced to wear a school uniform.

The Democratic Republic of Congo was ruled by President Mobutu Sese Seko for 32 years. He lived a life of great luxury while his country lacked basic health care. After he was removed from power in 1997 civil war broke out and several African countries sent troops to support the government or the rebels.

Hutus and Tutsis

Rwanda and neighboring Burundi have two main groups, the Hutus and the Tutsis. Both countries have suffered from outbursts of savagery as one tribe attacked another.

Violence erupted in Burundi in 1993 when a Hutu was elected president after decades of domination by the minority Tutsi. The new president was assassinated, and thousands were killed during the political crisis.

In 1994 the Rwandan Hutus rose up after the death of their president in a mysterious plane crash and massacred about half of all the Tutsis living in Rwanda. The rest fled and later fought back and seized power from the Hutus. One million Rwandans died in this turmoil.

Manganese mine

Manganese is an important export in Gabon. It is used in the manufacture of steel.

Refugees

The troubles in Rwanda have left many people without homes. These Tutsi children playing on a tree live in a refugee camp in Niashishi, south Rwanda. More than 8,000 refugees live in the camp under French protection.

SOUTHERN AFRICA

T he southern tip of Africa is an area
of contrasts. It includes the cascades of
the Victoria Falls, the dry Kalahari Desert,
the plateau of Table Mountain, and the unique
wildlife of Madagascar. It is also a region rich in mineral
deposits. The region's wealthiest country, South Africa,
is the world's top producer of gold and diamonds.

Hard at work in the fields

Women in southern Africa usually cultivate the crops because most men work in industries. Young children spend the day in the fields with their mothers, sometimes strapped to their backs.

Gold and diamond mining

Gold and diamonds account for about one third of South Africa's export earnings. Diamonds were first discovered in 1867 near the Orange River. A few years later a huge diamond field was found at Kimberley. Diamonds look very plain when they are dug out of the rock. They only glitter and sparkle after expert cutting and polishing, and this is often done abroad. Gold deposits have been mined in South Africa since the 1800s. However, ore supplies are gradually diminishing, and the economy is becoming less dependent on the mining industry.

Apartheid

In 1948 apartheid laws were passed in South Africa to keep black Africans, coloreds (mixed race), and Asians apart from whites. The laws applied to work, education, housing, public transportation, and entertainment. Leaders of the antiapartheid African National Congress (ANC), including Nelson Mandela, were put in prison. Apartheid was criticized by the rest of the world, and many countries stopped trading with South Africa. A sporting and entertainment ban was also enforced.

Drilling for gold
This miner is using a drill to extract the gold-bearing rock from a mine near Johannesburg.

Eventually the all-white government realized that the country could not continue this way. In 1990 President F. W. de Klerk scrapped apartheid and released Mandela from prison. In the elections of 1994 the black majority was allowed to vote for the first time. The ANC was voted into power, and Mandela was elected president.

Huge changes have taken place in South Africa since 1994, but it has also been a difficult time. People of all ethnic groups have been encouraged to talk about, but also forgive, the crimes of the apartheid era in the hope that all people can live and work together in peace. Many of its black citizens, after years of living in poverty, had high hopes that a better life would come quickly. They have been disappointed, and crime has risen sharply as a result. But hope remains that South Africa can work as a modern industrial country with opportunities for all of its citizens.

The fight for independence

Other southern African countries have struggled to gain their independence from European colonizers. In Zimbabwe white settlers took power in 1965 and declared independence from Great Britain. They fought a long and bitter civil war with black African rebels. Rebel leader Robert Mugabe eventually took power. But violence flared again from the late 1990s when President Mugabe began to confiscate land owned by white farmers.

A Communist government took over in Mozambique, but it had to fight a civil war with guerrilla forces backed by South Africa and Zimbabwe. Peace finally came in 1992.

Namibia was the last to gain independence—in 1990—but only after a long armed struggle against South African control.

Black leader
Nelson Mandela was president of South Africa from 1994 to 1999. He encouraged forgiveness for those who imposed apartheid.

A cultural inheritance

Over the past 100 years more and more people in southern Africa have moved to towns in search of jobs. Even so, two thirds of the people in the region still live in the country in small villages of grass-thatched, mud houses. Here they grow cereals, such as sorghum and corn, as well as beans and sweet potatoes. Often the electricity supply is unreliable. At night small lamps burn paraffin or kerosene, and wood provides heat for cooking. Some children have to walk long distances every day just to go to school.

The oldest inhabitants of the region are the San people, who have been living in the stony Kalahari Desert of Namibia and Botswana for 30,000 years. Much of their land has now been encroached on by international mining and agricultural corporations. However, some of the San people still survive by hunting for meat, gathering wild roots and berries, and storing water in ostrich egg shells.

Music and dance play a major part in the cultural life of southern Africa. Drumming is traditional at Zulu festivals in South Africa. In Mozambique the influence of the country's former Portuguese rulers can be heard in the rhythms of the guitar. And throughout southern Africa you can hear a very unusual instrument, the thumb piano. It consists of a small, wooden, handheld sound box with a row of metal prongs and produces twanging notes that are used as an accompaniment to singing.

The two tiny countries of Lesotho and Swaziland (Africa's smallest state) are both monarchies. Coronations and royal marriages are celebrated with drumming and warrior dances. The king of Swaziland's most important job is to bless the harvest. Every year, at the Festival of Incwala, the king emerges from his palace to perform a ritual dance before his people. He then takes a bite of food, signaling for the feasting to begin.

Art house

Folk art is not confined to museums—it is part of everyday life in southern Africa. The Ndebele women paint the outside of their homes with bright geometric patterns.

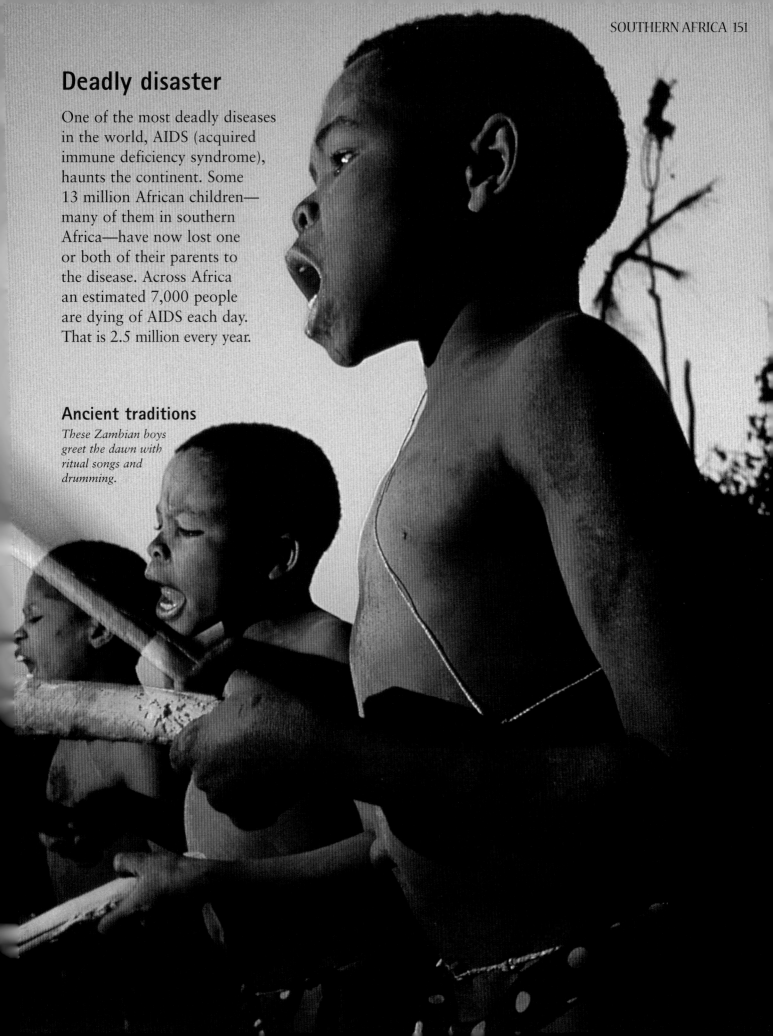

Deadly disaster

One of the most deadly diseases in the world, AIDS (acquired immune deficiency syndrome), haunts the continent. Some 13 million African children—many of them in southern Africa—have now lost one or both of their parents to the disease. Across Africa an estimated 7,000 people are dying of AIDS each day. That is 2.5 million every year.

Ancient traditions

These Zambian boys greet the dawn with ritual songs and drumming.

ALGERIA

Capital
Algiers
Area
918,500 sq. mi.
Population
31,736,053
Population density
35 per sq. mi.
Life expectancy
69 (m); 71 (f)
Religion
Islam
Languages
Arabic, French, Berber
dialects
Adult literacy rate
62 percent
Currency
Algerian dinar

 ANGOLA

Capital
Luanda
Area
480,800 sq. mi.
Population
10,366,031
Population density
22 per sq. mi.
Life expectancy
37 (m); 40 (f)
Religions
Traditional beliefs,
Christianity
Languages
Portuguese, Umbundo,
Bantu, Kimbundo,
Chokwe, Ganguela
Adult literacy rate
40 percent
Currency
Readjusted kwanza

 **BENIN**

Capital
Porto-Novo
Area
42,700 sq. mi.
Population
6,590,782
Population density
154 per sq. mi.
Life expectancy
49 (m); 50 (f)
Religions
Christianity, Islam,
traditional beliefs
Languages
French, Bariba, Fulani,
Fon, Yoruba
Adult literacy rate
37 percent
Currency
CFA franc

 BOTSWANA

Capital
Gaborone
Area
225,700 sq. mi.
Population
1,586,119
Population density
7 per sq. mi.
Life expectancy
37 (m); 38 (f)
Religions
Christianity, traditional beliefs
Languages
English, Setswana
Adult literacy rate
70 percent
Currency
Pula

 BURKINA-FASO

Capital
Ouagadougou
Area
105,600 sq. mi.
Population
12,272,289
Population density
116 per sq. mi.
Life expectancy
46 (m); 47 (f)
Religions
Islam, traditional beliefs,
Christianity
Languages
French, Mossi, and Sudanic
tribal languages
Adult literacy rate
19 percent
Currency
CFA franc

 **BURUNDI**

Capital
Bujumbura
Area
9,900 sq. mi.
Population
6,223,897
Population density
629 per sq. mi.
Life expectancy
45 (m); 47 (f)
Religions
Christianity, traditional beliefs
Languages
French, Kirundi, Swahili
Adult literacy rate
35 percent
Currency
Burundi franc

CAMEROON

Capital
Yaoundé
Area
181,000 sq. mi.
Population
15,803,220
Population density
87 per sq. mi.
Life expectancy
54 (m); 55 (f)
Religions
Traditional beliefs,
Christianity, Islam
Languages
English, French, and
local languages
Adult literacy rate
63 percent
Currency
CFA franc

 CAPE VERDE

Capital
Praia
Area
1,600 sq. mi.
Population
405,163
Population density
261 per sq. mi.
Life expectancy
66 (m); 73 (f)
Religion
Christianity
Languages
Portuguese, Crioulo
Adult literacy rate
72 percent
Currency
Cape Verdean escudo

 **CENTRAL AFRICAN REPUBLIC**

Capital
Bangui
Area
240,200 sq. mi.
Population
3,576,884
Population density
15 per sq. mi.
Life expectancy
42 (m); 45 (f)
Religions
Christianity, traditional
beliefs, Islam
Languages
French, Sangho, Arabic,
Hunsa, Swahili
Adult literacy rate
60 percent
Currency
CFA franc

 CHAD

Capital
N'Djamena
Area
485,600 sq. mi.
Population
8,707,078
Population density
18 per sq. mi.
Life expectancy
49 (m); 53 (f)
Religions
Islam, Christianity,
traditional beliefs
Languages
French, Arabic, Saro, Sango,
and local languages
Adult literacy rate
48 percent
Currency
CFA franc

 COMOROS

Capital
Moroni
Area
800 sq. mi.
Population
596,202
Population density
745 per sq. mi.
Life expectancy
58 (m); 63 (f)
Religions
Islam, Christianity
Languages
Comorian (Swahili and
Arabic), French, Arabic
Adult literacy rate
57 percent
Currency
Comoros franc

 DEMOCRATIC REPUBLIC OF THE CONGO

Capital
Kinshasa
Area
874,500 sq. mi.
Population
53,624,718
Population density
61 per sq. mi.
Life expectancy
47 (m); 51 (f)
Religions
Christianity, Islam,
traditional beliefs
Languages
French, Lingala, Kingwana,
Tshiluba, and local languages
Adult literacy rate
77 percent
Currency
Congolese franc

DJIBOUTI

Capital
Djibouti
Area
8,500 sq. mi.
Population
460,700
Population density
54 per sq. mi.
Life expectancy
49 (m); 53 (f)
Religions
Islam, Christianity
Languages
Arabic, French, Afar, Somali
Adult literacy rate
46 percent
Currency
Djibouti franc

 EGYPT

Capital
Cairo
Area
383,900 sq. mi.
Population
69,536,644
Population density
181 per sq. mi.
Life expectancy
62 (m); 66 (f)
Religions
Islam, Christianity
Languages
Arabic, English, French
Adult literacy rate
51 percent
Currency
Egyptian pound

 **EQUATORIAL GUINEA**

Capital
Malabo
Area
10,800 sq. mi.
Population
486,060
Population density
45 per sq. mi.
Life expectancy
52 (m); 56 (f)
Religion
Christianity
Languages
Spanish, French, Fang,
Bubi, and local languages
Adult literacy rate
78 percent
Currency
CFA franc

 ERITREA

Capital
Asmara
Area
46,800 sq. mi.
Population
4,298,269
Population density
92 per sq. mi.
Life expectancy
54 (m); 59 (f)
Religions
Islam, Christianity
Languages
Arabic, Tigre and Kunama,
Afar, Amhanc
Adult literacy rate
20 percent
Currency
Birr

 ETHIOPIA

Capital
Addis Ababa
Area
431,800 sq. mi.
Population
65,891,874
Population density
153 per sq. mi.
Life expectancy
44 (m); 46 (f)
Religions
Islam, Christianity,
traditional beliefs
Languages
Amharic, Tigrinya, Orominga
Adult literacy rate
35 percent
Currency
Birr

 GABON

Capital
Libreville
Area
99,400 sq. mi.
Population
1,221,175
Population density
12 per sq. mi.
Life expectancy
48 (m); 51 (f)
Religion
Christianity
Languages
French, Bantu dialects
Adult literacy rate
63 percent
Currency
CFA franc

GAMBIA, THE

Capital
Banjul
Area
3,900 sq. mi.
Population
1,411,205
Population density
366 per sq. mi.
Life expectancy
52 (m); 56 (f)
Religions
Islam, Christianity
Languages
English, Mandinka, Fula,
Wolof, and other local
languages
Adult literacy rate
39 percent
Currency
Dalasi

 GHANA

Capital
Accra
Area
88,700 sq. mi.
Population
19,894,014
Population density
224 per sq. mi.
Life expectancy
56 (m); 59 (f)
Religions
Traditional beliefs, Islam,
Christianity
Languages
Akan, Moshi-Dagomba,
Ewe, Ga
Adult literacy rate
64 percent
Currency
Cedi

 GUINEA

Capital
Conakry
Area
94,800 sq. mi.
Population
7,613,870
Population density
80 per sq. mi.
Life expectancy
44 (m); 48 (f)
Religions
Islam, Christianity
Languages
French, Soussou, Manika,
and other local languages
Adult literacy rate
36 percent
Currency
Guinean franc

 GUINEA-BISSAU

Capital
Bissau
Area
10,800 sq. mi.
Population
1,315,833
Population density
122 per sq. mi.
Life expectancy
47 (m); 52 (f)
Religions
Traditional beliefs, Islam,
Christianity
Languages
Portuguese, Creole
Adult literacy rate
55 percent
Currency
CFA franc

 IVORY COAST (CÔTE D'IVOIRE)

Capital
Yamoussoukro (official);
Abidjan (de facto)
Area
122,600 sq. mi.
Population
16,393,221
Population density
134 per sq. mi.
Life expectancy
44 (m); 46 (f)
Religions
Islam, traditional beliefs,
Christianity
Languages
French, Dioula, and local
languages
Adult literacy rate
40 percent
Currency
CFA franc

 **KENYA**

Capital
Nairobi
Area
219,500 sq. mi.
Population
30,765,916
Population density
140 per sq. mi.
Life expectancy
47 (m); 48 (f)
Religions
Christianity, traditional beliefs
Languages
Swahili, English, Kikuyu, Luo
Adult literacy rate
78 percent
Currency
Kenyan shilling

LESOTHO

Capital
Maseru
Area
11,700 sq. mi.
Population
2,177,062
Population density
186 per sq. mi.
Life expectancy
48 (m); 50 (f)
Religions
Christianity, traditional beliefs
Languages
English, Sesotho
Adult literacy rate
71 percent
Currency
Maloti

 **LIBERIA**

Capital
Monrovia
Area
37,100 sq. mi.
Population
3,225,837
Population density
87 per sq. mi.
Life expectancy
50 (m); 53 (f)
Religions
Traditional beliefs, Islam, Christianity
Languages
English and many local languages
Adult literacy rate
38 percent
Currency
Liberian dollar

LIBYA

Capital
Tripoli
Area
678,600 sq. mi.
Population
5,240,599
Population density
8 per sq. mi.
Life expectancy
74 (m); 78 (f)
Religion
Islam
Languages
Arabic, English, Italian
Adult literacy rate
76 percent
Currency
Libyan dinar

 MADAGASCAR

Capital
Antananarivo
Area
224,300 sq. mi.
Population
15,982,563
Population density
271 per sq. mi.
Life expectancy
53 (m); 58 (f)
Religions
Christianity, traditional beliefs, Islam
Languages
Malagasy, French, Hova, and other local languages
Adult literacy rate
46 percent
Currency
Malagasy franc

 MALAWI

Capital
Lilongwe
Area
36,300 sq. mi.
Population
10,548,250
Population density
291 per sq. mi.
Life expectancy
37 (m); 38 (f)
Religions
Christianity, Islam
Languages
English, Chichewa, and other local languages
Adult literacy rate
56 percent
Currency
Malawian kwacha

 MALI

Capital
Bamako
Area
470,500 sq. mi.
Population
11,008,578
Population density
23 per sq. mi.
Life expectancy
46 (m); 48 (f)
Religions
Islam, traditional beliefs
Languages
French, Bambara, and 12 other official languages
Adult literacy rate
31 percent
Currency
CFA franc

MAURITANIA

Capital
Nouakchott
Area
397,400 sq. mi.
Population
2,747,312
Population density
7 per sq. mi.
Life expectancy
49 (m); 53 (f)
Religion
Islam
Languages
Hasaniya, Arabic, Wolof,
Pular, Soninke
Adult literacy rate
38 percent
Currency
Ouguiya

 MAURITIUS

Capital
Port Louis
Area
700 sq. mi.
Population
1,189,825
Population density
1,169 per sq. mi.
Life expectancy
67 (m); 75 (f)
Religions
Hinduism, Christianity, Islam
Languages
English, Creole, French,
Hindi, Bojpoor
Adult literacy rate
83 percent
Currency
Mauritian rupee

 MOROCCO

Capital
Rabat
Area
172,100 sq. mi.
Population
30,645,305
Population density
178 per sq. mi.
Life expectancy
67 (m); 72 (f)
Religion
Islam
Languages
Arabic, Berber dialects,
Spanish, French
Adult literacy rate
44 percent
Currency
Moroccan dirham

 MOZAMBIQUE

Capital
Maputo
Area
302,400 sq. mi.
Population
19,371,057
Population density
64 per sq. mi.
Life expectancy
37 (m); 36 (f)
Religions
Christianity, Islam,
traditional beliefs
Languages
Portuguese and local
languages
Adult literacy rate
40 percent
Currency
Metical

 NAMIBIA

Capital
Windhoek
Area
317,500 sq. mi.
Population
1,797,677
Population density
6 per sq. mi.
Life expectancy
42 (m); 39 (f)
Religion
Christianity
Languages
English, Afrikaans, German,
and local languages
Adult literacy rate
62 percent
Currency
Namibian rand

 NIGER

Capital
Niamey
Area
488,500 sq. mi.
Population
10,355,156
Population density
21 per sq. mi.
Life expectancy
42 (m); 41 (f)
Religion
Islam
Languages
French, Hausa, Djerma
Adult literacy rate
14 percent
Currency
CFA franc

NIGERIA

Capital
Abuja
Area
351,200 sq. mi.
Population
126,635,626
Population density
361 per sq. mi.
Life expectancy
51 (m); 51 (f)
Religions
Islam, Christianity
Languages
English, Hausa, Yoruba, Ibo
Adult literacy rate
57 percent
Currency
Naira

 **REPUBLIC OF CONGO**

Capital
Brazzaville
Area
131,700 sq. mi.
Population
2,894,336
Population density
22 per sq. mi.
Life expectancy
44 (m); 51 (f)
Religions
Christianity, traditional
beliefs, Islam
Languages
French, Kikongo, Lingala,
and other local languages
Adult literacy rate
75 percent
Currency
CFA franc

RWANDA

Capital
Kigali
Area
9,600 sq. mi.
Population
7,312,756
Population density
760 per sq. mi.
Life expectancy
38 (m); 40 (f)
Religions
Christianity, traditional beliefs
Languages
French, English, Kinyarwanda,
Adult literacy rate
60 percent
Currency
Rwandan franc

 **SAO TOMÉ AND PRINCIPE**

Capital
São Tomé
Area
400 sq. mi.
Population
165,034
Population density
413 per sq. mi.
Life expectancy
64 (m); 67 (f)
Religion
Christianity
Languages
Portuguese, Mestico, and
local languages
Adult literacy rate
73 percent
Currency
Dobra

 SENEGAL

Capital
Dakar
Area
74,000 sq. mi.
Population
10,284,929
Population density
139 per sq. mi.
Life expectancy
61 (m); 64 (f)
Religions
Islam, traditional beliefs,
Christianity
Languages
French, Wolof, Pulaar, Diola,
Mandingo
Adult literacy rate
33 percent
Currency
CFA franc

 SEYCHELLES

Capital
Victoria
Area
176 sq. mi.
Population
79,715
Population density
453 per sq. mi.
Life expectancy
65 (m); 76 (f)
Religion
Christianity
Languages
English, French, Creole
Adult literacy rate
84 percent
Currency
Seychelles rupee

SIERRA LEONE

Capital
Freetown
Area
27,600 sq. mi.
Population
5,426,618
Population density
196 per sq. mi.
Life expectancy
43 (m); 49 (f)
Religions
Islam, traditional beliefs,
Christianity
Languages
English, Mende, Temne,
Krio (Creole)
Adult literacy rate
31 percent
Currency
Leone

 SOMALIA

Capital
Mogadishu
Area
241,900 sq. mi.
Population
7,488,773
Population density
31 per sq. mi.
Life expectancy
45 (m); 48 (f)
Religion
Islam
Languages
Somali, Arabic, English,
Italian
Adult literacy rate
24 percent
Currency
Somali shilling

 SOUTH AFRICA

Capital cities
Pretoria (administrative);
Cape Town (legislative);
Bloemfontein (judicial)
Area
470,900 sq. mi.
Population
43,586,097
Population density
93 per sq. mi.
Life expectancy
48 (m); 49 (f)
Religions
Christianity, Hinduism, Islam,
Languages
Afrikaans, English, and nine
African languages
Adult literacy rate
82 percent
Currency
South African rand

 SUDAN

Capital
Khartoum
Area
916,300 sq. mi.
Population
36,080,373
Population density
39 per sq. mi.
Life expectancy
56 (m); 58 (f)
Religions
Islam, Christianity
Languages
Arabic, Nubian,
Ta Bedawie
Adult literacy rate
46 percent
Currency
Sudanese dinar

 SWAZILAND

Capital
Mbabane (administrative);
Lobamba (legislative)
Area
6,600 sq. mi.
Population
1,104,343
Population density
166 per sq. mi.
Life expectancy
38 (m); 39 (f)
Religions
Christianity, traditional beliefs
Languages
English, Siswati
Adult literacy rate
77 percent
Currency
Lilangeni

 TANZANIA

Capital
Dodoma
Area
341,700 sq. mi.
Population
36,232,074
Population density
106 per sq. mi.
Life expectancy
51 (m); 53 (f)
Religions
Christianity, Islam,
traditional beliefs
Languages
Swahili, English, and
local languages
Adult literacy rate
68 percent
Currency
Tanzanian shilling

 **TOGO**

Capital
Lomé
Area
21,000 sq. mi.
Population
5,153,088
Population density
246 per sq. mi.
Life expectancy
52 (m); 56 (f)
Religions
Traditional beliefs,
Christianity, Islam
Languages
French, Ewe, Mina,
Dagomba, Kabye
Adult literacy rate
52 percent
Currency
CFA franc

 TUNISIA

Capital
Tunis
Area
59,900 sq. mi.
Population
9,705,102
Population density
162 per sq. mi.
Life expectancy
72 (m); 76 (f)
Religion
Islam
Languages
Arabic, French
Adult literacy rate
67 percent
Currency
Tunisian dinar

 **UGANDA**

Capital
Kampala
Area
77,000 sq. mi.
Population
23,985,712
Population density
311 per sq. mi.
Life expectancy
43 (m); 44 (f)
Religions
Christianity, traditional
beliefs, Islam
Languages
English, Luganda, Swahili
Adult literacy rate
62 percent
Currency
Ugandan shilling

 ZAMBIA

Capital
Lusaka
Area
285,700 sq. mi.
Population
9,770,199
Population density
34 per sq. mi.
Life expectancy
37 (m); 38 (f)
Religions
Christianity, traditional
beliefs, Hinduism, Islam
Languages
English, Bemba, Kaonda,
Lozi, Tonga, and other
local languages
Adult literacy rate
78 percent
Currency
Zambian kwacha

 ZIMBABWE

Capital
Harare
Area
149,100 sq. mi.
Population
11,365,366
Population density
376 per sq. mi.
Life expectancy
39 (m); 36 (f)
Religions
Christianity, traditional beliefs
Languages
English, Shona, Sindebele,
and other local languages
Adult literacy rate
85 percent
Currency
Zimbabwe dollar

ASIA

Severnaya Zemlya

Kara Sea

Taymyr Peninsula

Yamal Peninsula

Gydan Peninsula

Central Siberian Plateau

West Siberian Plain

Ural Mountains

Irtysh

Ob.

Yenisey

RUSSIAN FEDERATION

(Capital Moscow)

Black Sea

ANKARA

TURKEY

GEORGIA

T'bilisi

CYPRUS
Nicosia

ARMENIA

Yerevan

AZERBAIJAN

Baku

Beirut

LEBANON

Jerusalem

Damascus

SYRIA

ISRAEL

JORDAN

Amman

Euphrates

Baghdad

IRAQ

Tigris

Caspian Sea

TURKMENISTAN

Ashgabat

TEHRAN

IRAN

Iranian Plateau

KUWAIT

Kuwait

The Gulf

Riyadh

**SAUDI
ARABIA**

Al Manamah
BAHRAIN
Doha

QATAR

Abu Dhabi

U.A.E.

Arabian Peninsula

Muscat

Sana

Red Sea

YEMEN

OMAN

Gulf of Aden

Socotra

KAZAKHSTAN

Astana

Aral Sea

UZBEKISTAN

Tashkent

Bishkek

KYRGYZSTAN

Dushanbe

TAJIKISTAN

Hindu Kush

Kabul

AFGHANISTAN

Islamabad

KASHMIR
Administered
by Pakistan

K2
△28,244 ft.

AKSAI
Administered
by China

PAKISTAN

Indus

Thar Desert

New Delhi

Lake Balkhash

Ulan Bato

MONGOLI

Altai

Tian Shan

Pik Pobedy
24,403 ft.

Taklimakan

Kuntun Shan

Plateau
of Tibet

CHIN

Gobi Desert

HIMALAYAS

Mt. Everest
29,021 ft.
△

NEPAL

Kathmandu

BHUTAN
Thimphu

Brahmaputra

Ganges

BANGLADESH

Dhaka

Irrawaddy

INDIA

Deccan Plateau

Bay of Bengal

MYANMAR

LAOS

Vientiane

Yangoon
(Rangoon)

THAILAND

Bangko

CAMB

Phnom Pe

Arabian Sea

Laccadive Is.

MALDIVES

Male

SRI LANKA

Colombo

Andaman Is.

Andaman Sea

Gulf of Thailand

Nicobar Is.

MALAYSIA

Kuala Lumpur

Singapore

Sumatra

INDIAN

OCEAN

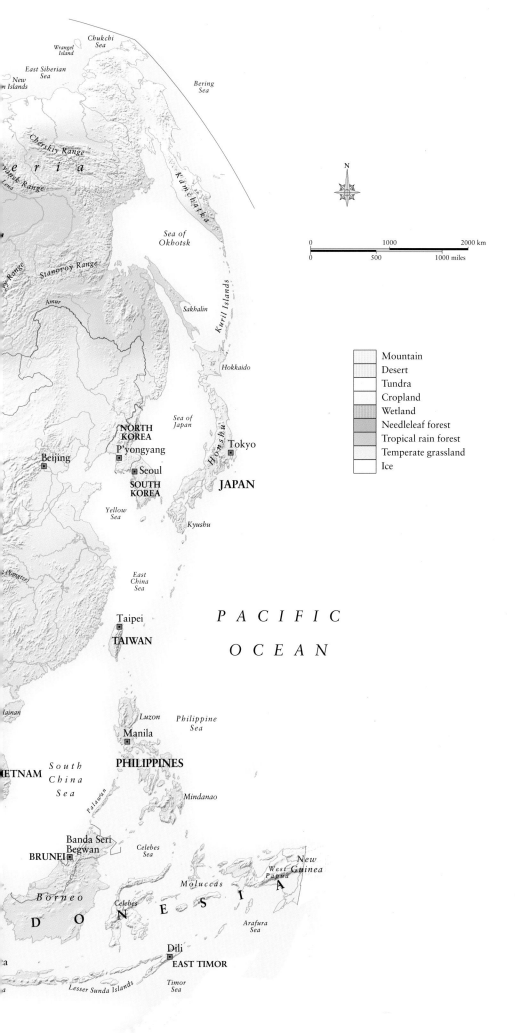

Wrangel Island

Chukchi Sea

East Siberian Sea

New n Islands

Cherskiy Range

i a

Lena

Range

nskiy Range

Bering Sea

Kamchatka

Sea of Okhotsk

Stanovoy Range

Amur

Range

Sakhalin

Kuril Islands

Hokkaido

Sea of Japan

Honshu

NORTH KOREA

P'yongyang

□ Tokyo

Beijing

□ Seoul

SOUTH KOREA

JAPAN

Yellow Sea

Kyushu

(Yangtze)

East China Sea

Taipei

TAIWAN

P A C I F I C

O C E A N

Hainan

Luzon

Philippine Sea

Manila

South China Sea

PHILIPPINES

ETNAM

Palawan

Mindanao

Banda Seri Begwan

Celebes Sea

BRUNEI

New Guinea

West Papua

Borneo

Moluccas

D O N E S I A

Celebes

Arafura Sea

Dili

EAST TIMOR

Lesser Sunda Islands

Timor Sea

N

0   1000   2000 km

0   500   1000 miles

Mountain
Desert
Tundra
Cropland
Wetland
Needleleaf forest
Tropical rain forest
Temperate grassland
Ice

Ring of fire

Japan lies on the Pacific "ring of fire," making it vulnerable to volcanic eruptions, earthquakes, and tsunamis.

Financial city

The Chinese city of Hong Kong was under British rule until 1997 when it was returned to China. It is a financial center with major world banks, and it is China's most crowded city.

India

The Indian subcontinent is separated from the rest of Asia by the Himalayas. India is the world's second most populous country after China. The U.S. is the third most populous.

Oil rich

Middle East countries, such as Saudi Arabia and Kuwait, have huge gas and oil reserves, which they export.

Western and southern Asia
THE MIDDLE EAST

The world's first cities developed about 5,500 years ago in the area between the Tigris and Euphrates rivers. This region, called Mesopotamia, lies mainly in what is now Iraq. Much of the land is dry, but these early civilizations dug irrigation canals to direct the river water onto their crops. Water is still a precious commodity—perhaps more precious even than oil, which has brought great wealth to many countries in the region.

Camel racing

Today camels are more likely to be bred for racing than as beasts of burden. A big race at Dubai's racetrack may have up to 50 runners. To keep the weight down, the jockeys are usually young boys.

The Bedouins

A large area of southern Saudi Arabia is known as the Empty Quarter because it contains little but shifting sand dunes. It is one of the most hostile environments on earth, but the Bedouins can survive there. This would be impossible except for their camels, which can travel for two weeks without eating or drinking. The camels carry all the Bedouins' supplies, including tents, rugs and bedding, skins full of water, and food such as bread, dates, and goat cheese. The camels provide milk to drink and to make into yogurt. They also supply meat, wool, leather, and dung to burn as fuel. The Bedouins move around the desert with their flocks of sheep and herds of goats, using their skills to find pastures and vital waterholes.

Oases

Wherever there is sufficient water, settlements have sprung up in the desert, allowing people to live and grow dates, pumpkins, onions, and figs. They also grow wheat, which is used to make flat bread. Goats and chickens are raised for food—but not pigs because pork is forbidden by Islam.

Some oases are huge. Riyadh, the capital and largest city of Saudi Arabia with a population of 1.8 million, is an oasis. So, too, is Damascus, the capital of Syria and the world's oldest continuously inhabited city, dating back some 4,500 years.

Mountain farmers

Not all of the land in the Middle East is desert. Where there are hills and mountains there is usually enough rainfall to turn the landscape green. Most of the people of Yemen live in the hills that line the Red Sea coast in the west. Here they can grow wheat, vegetables, cotton, and coffee.

Much of Lebanon is mountainous. The best farmland is in the hills and in the Bekaa Valley in the Lebanon Mountains. All kinds of vegetables can be grown here, such as onions, tomatoes, and eggplant, as well as citrus fruits, olives, and almonds. In the Elburz Mountains of northern Iran the rivers are lined with ribbons of green farmland, but the summer heat creates bare, rocky desert wherever the land is beyond the reach of water.

Summers are hot throughout the region, and a big problem facing farmers is drought. The heat evaporates water before plants can absorb it. For every liter absorbed by plants, five liters may evaporate into the air.

Three world religions

The region at the eastern end of the Mediterranean, covering Israel and Syria, is known as the Holy Land to Jews and Christians. It includes Canaan, the "promised land" of Abraham, where most of the events of the Old Testament took place. Israel is where Jesus was born and preached his message. Islam developed in the west of Saudi Arabia, in the prophet Muhammad's home city of Mecca and the city of Medina, 217 mi. (350km) to the north of Mecca. After Muhammad's death in A.D. 632 his followers spread Islam far and wide, mainly by conquest. As a result, Islam is now the main religion and Arabic the main language of the Middle East.

Islam is divided into two main branches— Shiism and Sunnism. Most Muslims are Sunnis, but the Iranians are Shiites. A revolution led by Ayatollah Khomeini overthrew the rule of the Shah (king) in 1979. Since then the Islamic government of Iran has applied a strict interpretation of Islamic law, restricting the Western style of life that developed during the Shah's reign. Women could no longer be seen in public in jeans, for example, and had to cover themselves in a chador (a black, hooded robe).

The Torah

These Jews are carrying a copy of the Torah, a handwritten scroll containing the laws of Judaism.

The Diaspora

Although Israel is the Jewish Holy Land, most Jews were pushed out in ancient times. They were forced to settle abroad by foreign conquerors such as the Romans. This scattering of the nation was called the Diaspora. In the 1800s Jews began lobbying for the

Protest march

These Palestinian children carry portraits of Palestinian leader Yasser Arafat and 14-year-old A'la Jawabreh, who was killed by gunfire in a refugee camp near Hebron in 2000.

creation of a new Jewish state in what was then called Palestine. Jewish settlers returned to these lands, and after World War II they fought for their own nation, declaring an independent state of Israel in 1948. This went against the wishes of the Muslim Palestinians already living there. Four wars followed as neighboring Arab countries tried to force out the Jews in favor of the Palestinians, but they failed each time.

In 1994 the Palestinians were given limited self-rule over parts of the West Bank (of the Jordan River) and the Gaza Strip (along the Mediterranean coast). But many Palestinians still fight for a better settlement.

This ongoing struggle remains the greatest cause of friction in the Middle East and throughout the Muslim world.

Turkish mosque

This mosque in southern Turkey looks out over the landscape of Syria. Modern Turkey does not have a state religion, but it was once strictly a Muslim country. Recently there has been a revival of interest in Islamic culture.

A precious resource

The lack of water has always been a problem for the Middle East. In the past clever systems were developed to carry it across the land. In Iran *foggaras* (large tunnels) were dug beneath the desert to bring water to oases from mountain springs 31 mi. (50km) away. In Syria huge waterwheels lifted water from the Orontes River to supply crops in the fields. Some of these medieval wheels still survive.

Today there are many more people living in the Middle East and an even greater demand for water. In the Gulf States freshwater is made from seawater processed in desalination plants (the salt is taken out). Israel imports water from Turkey by ship, but this supplies only five percent of the country's needs.

Water is so precious that it can be the cause of disputes. One third of Israel's freshwater comes from Lake Kinneret. The source of that water is the Golan Heights, which Israel captured from Syria in the Six Day War of 1967. The area remains in dispute by the two countries.

Wealth from oil

Many Middle Eastern countries have valuable oil reserves—Saudi Arabia, Iran, Iraq, Oman, Yemen, and the tiny Gulf States of Kuwait, Qatar, Bahrain, and the United Arab Emirates. Wealth from oil has allowed these nations to improve their cities and has funded new hospitals and banks.

Old Arab traditions have been strengthened by this new money. Modern buildings have been designed in Islamic style, with arches, domes, and decorative tiles. Traditional Arab music is supported by wealthy sponsors and by the new radio and television stations.

Fearing that one day their oil will run out, many countries have invested in new projects. Bahrain, for example, processes aluminum and manufactures machinery and electrical goods.

Oil refinery

This oil refinery in Kuwait is one of many in the Persian Gulf. Huge tankers pick up oil from coastal terminals, making the Gulf one of the world's busiest seaways.

THE MIDDLE EAST 169

Traditional dress

In the Gulf States the traditional dress for men is a dishdasha (a flowing cotton gown). They also wear a headdress to keep off the heat.

An unstable region

Desert golf course

In the wealthy United Arab Emirates money from oil has been used to create this golf course in the desert.

Many Middle Eastern countries are ruled by royal families, with kings, sultans, or emirs at the head. The rich are fabulously rich, while the poor live well below the poverty line. Islam plays a strong role in government, but Muslim fundamentalists want even stricter Islamic laws, and despite its great wealth, the Middle East is a tense and unstable region.

CENTRAL ASIA

In 1991 the former Soviet Union broke up. A group of countries in the middle of the Asian continent broke away from Russia and became independent nations for the first time in modern history. They cover a vast region and all kinds of landscapes and climates, from the desert of Turkmenistan to the grasslands of Kazakhstan and the mountains of Kyrgyzstan.

The steppes

Kazakhstan is five times larger than France and almost the size of India. Much of its landscape is covered in grasslands—the steppes. Nomadic herders roam across the steppes on horseback with their herds of cattle and flocks of sheep. They live in yurts (round, felt tents). The Kazakh traditional food is koumiss, a drink made from fermented mare's milk.

In modern times it has become increasingly hard for the Kazakh herders to make a living from raising livestock. Many have been forced to grow crops or move to the cities to find work in the factories.

The Silk Road

The central Asian nations lie on the ancient trade route between Asia and Europe known as the Silk Road. The cities of Tashkent, Samarkand, and Kiva in Uzbekistan were trading centers along this route. These cities are still full of merchants and traders. Bazaars and stalls sell fruit, spices, silk, and cotton.

The Silk Road carried not only goods but also ideas and cultures. A mix of nationalities has developed, each with its own identity and language. The people of Kazakhstan, for example, are descendants of Turk and Mongol settlers and speak Kazakh.

Riding skills
The children of Kazakh herders learn to ride at a very early age and spend much of their lives on horseback.

Religious differences

Islam was brought to central Asia in the A.D. 600s and is the main religion today. However, to the west of the Caspian Sea there is mix of religious faiths. The people of Azerbaijan are mostly Muslims, but in neighboring Armenia, Christianity is the dominant religion. This mix has been the cause of political tension.

In the early 1990s a bitter civil war broke out between Armenia and Azerbaijan over Nagorno-Karabakh. This region lies within the borders of Muslim Azerbaijan, but most of its population is Christian and Armenian. A ceasefire was declared in 1994, but the dispute has left 20 percent of Azerbaijan under Armenian control.

Georgia is a mountainous country where four fifths of the people are Christians. There is an ongoing armed struggle with the Muslim population of Abkhazia in the west of the country. They want independence from Georgia.

Everyday life

Most people in the central Asian republics live in modest homes in villages and towns and struggle to make a living. The cities are developing fast, however, as traders and industrialists from all over the world seek new business opportunities. But many skilled Russians have moved back to Russia. Standards of health care, schooling, and housing have become worse as a result.

Farming and industry

In mountainous Uzbekistan, Tajikistan, and Kyrgyzstan farmers cultivate the river valleys. In the fertile Fergana Valley of Uzbekistan they grow fruit, rice, and cotton.

They also breed silkworms for their cocoons, which are used to make silk. In the sheltered valleys in Georgia farmers grow grapes to make wine.

Large-scale commercial farming was introduced in the Soviet era. The Soviets created elaborate irrigation systems, notably in Turkmenistan where farms take water from the Karakum Canal, which runs through the south of the country. The rivers flowing into the Aral Sea were used as a water source for the cotton fields in Uzbekistan, Kazakhstan, and Turkmenistan. The sea has now shrunk to half of its original size and is surrounded by infertile, salt-laden soil.

Fishing is important for those countries bordering the sea. The Caspian Sea is the world's main source of caviar—the eggs of

the sturgeon fish. Caviar is considered a gourmet food and is very expensive to buy—a 3.5 oz. (100g) can may cost more than $150.

During the Soviet era the Soviets also developed mines and set up industries in the region. Factories produce processed foods, textiles, clothing, machinery, and chemicals. But the most valuable products of all are oil and natural gas, found beneath the Caspian Sea off Kazakhstan, Turkmenistan, and in Azerbaijan. Baku, the capital of Azerbaijan, is now a major center of the oil industry.

Tourism is also developing in central Asia. The Tian Shan Mountains and the route of the Silk Road are popular attractions. But political unrest in the region deters many visitors.

Shrinking sea
The Aral Sea was once a major lake, supplying fish and water to the people living around its shores, but it has shrunk to half of its original size.

Cotton pickers
The annual cotton crop of Uzbekistan matches that of the U.S. Cotton is known as "white gold" in the region.

INDIA

Staple food

Rice is one of the staple foods in India. Rice fields, called paddies, are flooded at the start of the growing season. The seedlings are then planted by hand.

W ith around one billion people, India has the second largest population in the world, but the people only live in about one third of the land space. This results in the cities being overcrowded—trains and buses are often so packed with people that some passengers ride on the roofs!

People and worship

Within this large population there are many different languages spoken—Hindu and English are the official languages, with another 14 major languages spoken throughout the country. There are also 845 dialects—out of a world total of 3,950.

Most Indians are followers of Hinduism, an ancient religion with hundreds of gods and heroes, but India is the birthplace of several other religions as well. Buddhism began about 2,500 years ago when Siddhartha Gautama, who became known as the Buddha, left his wealthy family home and set out on a quest for truth. His teachings, which overturned many Hindu beliefs, spread across India.

Sikhism developed in the Punjab state in about A.D. 1500, combining many of the beliefs of Hinduism and Islam. Islam itself was introduced to India from A.D. 300. There are many other religions with smaller numbers of followers, for example Jainism and Zoroastrianism.

Sacred river

Hindus believe that certain rivers can wash away sins. The Ganges River is particularly sacred, and many people bathe in its waters.

A variety of spices

Indian cooking is famous all over the world. Complex flavors, spices, and the use of fiery-hot chilies are just some of its characteristics. Dishes of rice or bread with dal (puréed legumes), mildly spiced vegetables, and perhaps small quantities of meat or fish are served at mealtimes.

Food varies greatly from place to place. In southern India there are rice cakes and stews flavored with bananas. On the west coast around Goa meat is cooked with coconut milk. Tandoori food, baked in a clay oven, is very popular in the northwest.

Rice fields and tea leaves

The different climates and landscapes of India influence the types of food produced. Most of the rice is grown in the wetter, tropical climate of the coastal regions, and grain comes from the plains of northern India, especially near the Ganges River.

Darjeeling, in the foothills of the Himalaya mountains, and the fertile land of the northeastern state of Assam provide the perfect conditions to grow tea. India is the largest tea exporter in the world. Tea bushes are grown in huge plantations, and the leaves are picked by hand and placed in huge baskets carried on the tea pickers' backs.

Most of India is hot, and every year from June to September a rainy season sweeps in on the monsoon winds, producing hot and sticky weather. But this rarely touches the Thar Desert, which fills much of the northwest region bordering Pakistan. Millet, sorghum, and corn are grown on the edges of the desert, but the driest regions are home only to nomadic camel herders.

Two thirds of the Indian population live in small villages, making a living through farming. Many are employed by the large plantations, while others farm their own small plots of land.

Little princess

Sikhism is the religion of many people in the state of Punjab in northern India. Sikh girls take the last name "Kaur" (princess). Sikh boys are known as "Singh" (lion).

The caste system

Hinduism is not just a religion, it is a way of life. Hindu society was once divided into castes. At the top were the Brahmans, who were doctors, lawyers, teachers, and other professionals. Next came the Kshatriyas, the landowners and large-scale farmers. The third caste were the Vaisyas, the traders. The fourth were the Sudras, ordinary workers. Some people doing menial jobs, such as sweeping the streets and collecting the garbage, used to be outside the caste system. They lived apart from the rest of society and were known as "Untouchables." Today children are taught that the caste system is not acceptable.

Painted elephant

Ganesh, the god of prosperity, is portrayed as a man with an elephant's head. To represent Ganesh, real elephants are sometimes painted to take part in religious parades.

Street performers

Jugglers, musicians, snake charmers, and acrobats play to enthusiastic audiences in streets and marketplaces all over India.

It is not as strong as it used to be, but it still affects what jobs people do, who they marry, what they wear, and even what they eat.

Gods and festivals

The stories of Hindu gods are told in famous poems that are sung on special occasions. Brahma is the lord of all creation. Vishnu is the god who preserves life, and he is reborn on earth from time to time to fight evil and to protect mankind. Shiva represents all the forces of nature. The elephant-headed god Ganesh is thought to bring good luck and prosperity. His face can be seen on posters and calendars throughout India.

Hindu festivals are very colorful occasions. Statues of the gods are dressed up and decorated with gold. At the Festival of Holi people run around the streets, throwing powdered dye at each other. The dye symbolizes fertility. During Diwali, the festival of lights, lamps are lit in the doors and windows of every house and twinkle like thousands of little stars.

The most spectacular festival is the Kumbha Mela, held every 12 years at Allahabad, where two sacred rivers, the Jumna and the Ganges, merge. It is the world's largest festival, attended by 12 million people. Five days of celebrations begin with the procession of the sadhus (holy men who have given up all their possessions and live by begging).

Sports and entertainment

Cricket is the country's most popular sport, and children usually play it in the streets. When the Indian cricket team plays a test match against England, Australia, or Pakistan, millions tune in their radios to listen.

Watching plays is another popular pastime. Traveling theaters tour around the country performing plays based on current events in the news. In southern India the Kathakali performers retell stories from the Hindu sacred books wearing vivid make up and elaborate costumes. Shadow puppets are another traditional entertainment. They tell old stories using mime and sound.

Cricket hero

Saurav Ganguly was born in Calcutta in 1972. He started playing for India when he was still a teenager and later went on to captain the national team. He is considered to be one of India's greatest batsmen.

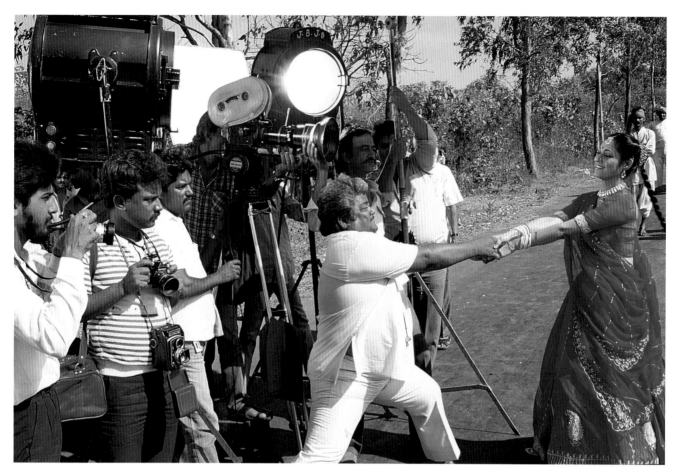

Bollywood

Mumbai (Bombay) is the center of India's huge movie industry, and it is known around the world by its nickname, "Bollywood." More movies are produced here than anywhere else in the world, including Hollywood.

Most Indian movies are musical romances, with choreographed fight scenes, spectacular song-and-dance routines, and larger-than-life villains and heroes.

The music is played on traditional instruments, such as the stringed sitar, which looks like a long-necked guitar, and the tabla drums. The tabla is a pair of drums consisting of a small, wooden right-hand drum and a larger, metal left-hand drum.

Bollywood movies are extremely popular throughout the Indian subcontinent, and the actors who star in them can become very rich and famous.

Film stars

Bollywood actors such as Tina Minum, shown here, are huge stars in India.

India today

After 200 years of British control India became independent in 1947. Its democratic, multiparty government is based on the British system.

Two thirds of the population live in villages, scraping by with farming. Others work in factories in huge cities, such as Delhi and Kolkata (Calcutta), making clothing, chemicals, machinery, or electrical equipment. India also has a growing computer industry.

Although some have become wealthy through business, the computer industry, or movies, the majority of people are poor, doing menial jobs with long hours and low pay. Children as young as five work on farms and in workshops. Their wages are essential to help feed their families.

PAKISTAN

In 1947 when India became independent from Great Britain Muslims wanted their own nation separate from the Hindus. British India was divided, with parts of the north becoming Pakistan. At first Pakistan had two parts: East and West. But in 1971 after a civil war East Pakistan broke free and became Bangladesh.

Ancient and modern

The Indus River and its tributaries flow through the dry Indus plain that extends across most of Pakistan. Thanks to their waters, one of the world's first civilizations grew up in the Indus Valley 5,000 years ago. Today the rivers provide water to irrigate the land in the province of Punjab, which is the main agricultural area. Wheat, sugarcane, vegetables, and fruits are produced. Rice, grown in flooded paddy fields, is a major export crop. Cotton is also grown here and is used in the textile industry.

Pakistan is a mix of old and new. In cities, such as Islamabad (the capital), there are high-rise buildings and shopping malls.

Apricot harvest

Women from the Hunza region of Pakistan sort freshly picked apricots and arrange them on circular mats to dry in the sun.

In the bazaars VCRs, pocket calculators, and Japanese watches are sold alongside fruits and vegetables, handmade rugs, and carpets. Music cassettes and CDs blare out modern versions of traditional music.

Pakistan is a Muslim country, and most women observe the Islamic rule of dressing modestly by wearing a veil to cover their head. Families are large, with an average of seven people in every household. Marriages are traditionally arranged by the family, although young Pakistanis are increasingly finding their own marriage partners.

Political troubles

Since the partition with India, Pakistan has been in dispute with its neighbor over Kashmir, a region in the far north. In 1947 the Hindu leader of Kashmir chose to join India rather than Pakistan, although most of the Kashmiri people are Muslim. The territory remains under Indian control, but it is still a bone of contention, leading to outbreaks of violence.

In 1971 East Pakistan demanded independence. After months of civil war it declared itself a new nation, Bangladesh.

Pakistan was again thrown into crisis in September 2001 when the U.S.-led attacks on neighboring Afghanistan threatened to upset Pakistan's stability. There were mass demonstrations against the U.S. attacks, but Pakistan's military government restrained the demonstrators and gave support to the U.S.

Language

There are several ethnic groups in Pakistan. The remote mountains in the north of the country are home to the Gujars, who live as nomadic herders. Many people who live on the border with Afghanistan are Pashtuns, who have a reputation as warriors. The people of the Punjab region are mainly farmers.

Urdu is the official language in Pakistan, but the different ethnic groups also have their own languages—Pashto, Punjabi, Sindhi, Saraiki, and Baluchi are spoken in different parts of the region.

Education

More than 40 percent of the population is under 15 years old. Education is free, but it is not mandatory. Only one third of the children of elementary school age go to school. Even so, classes are large, with more than 40 pupils to every teacher. This lack of schooling means that only 54 percent of men and 24 percent of women can read and write.

Schoolchildren

These schoolgirls in Karachi are learning to read and write. Even though schooling is free, some families choose not to educate their daughters.

THE REST OF SOUTHERN ASIA

The landmass made up of India and the neighboring countries is often called the Indian subcontinent. The north is hemmed in by the Himalaya mountains, and the south is surrounded by the tropical Indian Ocean. To the west is the high land of Afghanistan, and to the east is low-lying Bangladesh.

Nepal

Nepal lies in the Himalaya Mountains. In the north of the country, at 13,776 ft. (4,200m) above sea level, the people live by farming, growing grain and vegetables, and herding sheep and goats. They also keep yaks (long-haired cattle that can only live at this height). Yaks are used to carry goods along the

Buddhist temple

The eyes of the Buddha are painted on the four faces of the Bodnath Stupa in Nepal. Stupas are ancient burial mounds believed to contain relics of early holy men. Prayer flags flutter from lines attached to the stupa, scattering prayers into the wind.

mountain paths. They also provide milk, meat, and leather. The southern part of the country, which is not so mountainous, is the main agricultural region. Here the fertile soil produces rice and corn, vegetables, and fruit.

Most of the people are very poor and live in mud-brick or wooden houses. The capital, Kathmandu, which lies in the middle of Nepal at a height of 4,395 ft. (1,340m) above sea level, is the only city in a country of 25 million people.

Most people are Hindus, and some believe that the king is the reincarnation of the god Vishnu. Until 1990 monarchs had absolute power in the country. But nationwide unrest forced the king to accept a parliamentary system. In 2001 the crown prince assassinated his father and other members of the royal family and then shot himself. The king's brother took over, but the royal family's authority has been damaged.

Tourism is a valuable source of income. Visitors come on hiking expeditions or to climb in the Himalayas. Mount Everest (29,021 ft./8,848m) is the world's highest mountain. Local Sherpa people provide assistance as guides and porters.

Bhutan

To the east of Nepal, also bordering China, lies the tiny mountain kingdom of Bhutan. This is a devout Buddhist country, with 1,300 monasteries. Until 1998 the king ruled over the population of two million people with absolute power, preserving their traditional society by restricting visitors and banning Western influences such as television. The monarch, known as Druk Gyalpo ("dragon king"), now shares power with a government.

National dress is compulsory. Men wear a *gho* (a knee-length wraparound), and women wear a *kira* (an ankle-length dress). People live by herding yaks or by growing potatoes, wheat, and rice in the lowlands.

Bhutan shepherdess

This young Bhutanese girl is wearing a traditional kira. *Like most of the population, her family makes a living by farming.*

Jute harvest

Jute is grown in the wetlands of Bangladesh. The long, fibrous stems are used to make sacking and mats.

Delta country

To the south of Bhutan the land flattens out into the low plain occupied by Bangladesh. Two great rivers, the Brahmaputra and the Ganges, flow south from the Himalayas and cross the plain. Joined by the Meghna River in the east, they form numerous channels and create a huge delta that runs into the Bay of Bengal. This well-watered land is good for growing crops, but the rivers often flood their banks when the Himalayan snow melts in the spring and summer, causing floods. Worse still, the region is frequently hit by devastating storms called cyclones. These cause tidal waves that surge up the rivers and wash whole villages away. Many people have been killed by such disasters. In 1970 half a million people died beneath a 50-ft. (15-m) -high tidal wave. Bangladesh struggles to feed its population of 131 million people because of these natural disasters.

Three fourths of the population lives by farming—growing rice and vegetables. The most important export, however, is clothing. Foreign companies come to Bangladesh because the people work for low wages, which keeps the cost of the finished clothes down. More recently factories have produced high-tech television and computer components.

Millions of children work on farms and in factories, but the Bangladesh government and charities are doing much to end child labor and improve elementary education.

Refugees

After the terrorist attacks against the U.S. on September 11, 2001, thousands of Afghan people fled their homes in fear of a U.S. military response. They crossed the borders to Pakistan and Iran and stayed in refugee camps.

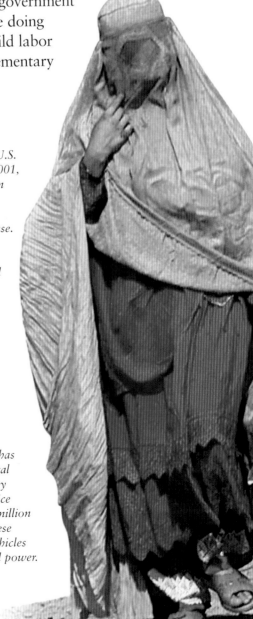

Traffic jam

There are more than 300,000 rickshas in Dhaka, the capital of Bangladesh. They provide a taxi service for the city's 12.3 million people. Most of these brightly colored vehicles are driven by pedal power.

War-torn Afghanistan

Afghanistan is inhabited by a number of mainly Muslim peoples who live by traditional farming, growing grains, fruits, and nuts in the river valleys and herding sheep in the sparse mountain pastures. It was a monarchy until 1973, when the army overthrew the king. This was the beginning of decades of unrest.

In 1979 the Soviet Union invaded Afghanistan to support a pro-communist regime that had seized power in a coup. For ten years it tried to conquer the country, fighting a vicious war against Islamic resistance fighters, the mujahideen (holy warriors). When the Soviet army finally withdrew, the Afghan people fought among themselves for control of the country. This civil war was brought to an end in the 1990s by the Taliban, who took control of almost all of the country and introduced a very strict kind of Islamic law and code of behavior.

All music, movies, and videos were banned. Women could not work for pay or be seen in public, except when covered from head to foot in the *burka* (a traditional robe). Children could not do anything that might distract them from religious studies such as flying kites or playing chess. Girls could not go to school.

The Taliban let a terrorist group called Al Qaeda, led by Osama bin Laden, build training camps in Afghanistan. Al Qaeda was suspected of destroying the World Trade Center in New York City and part of the Pentagon in Washington, D.C. on September 11, 2001. When the Taliban refused to hand over Bin Laden, a U.S.-led coalition launched war on the Taliban. Shortly after the U.S. began a bombing campaign the anti-Taliban Northern Alliance captured the capital, Kabul, and most of the country, and the Taliban was removed from power. A new coalition government was formed.

Tea pickers

The hills in the center of Sri Lanka are covered with tea bushes. Women pick the tea, selecting only the delicate, young shoots. These are rolled, dried, and heated and then packed in wooden chests for export.

Stilt fishermen

Villagers on the southwest coast of Sri Lanka perch on poles to do their fishing. Nobody knows how or why this strange technique originated, but stilts in good positions are much prized and are passed on from father to son.

Sri Lanka

Sri Lanka is a tropical island off the southeast coast of India. From the palm-fringed beaches that line the coast, the land rises to high hills that provide the perfect conditions for growing tea. The islanders also grow rubber trees, from which rubber is extracted, and cinnamon trees, the bark of which is peeled off to use as a cooking spice. Much of the southwest of the island is covered with rain forests, where timber is collected with the help of elephants. There are, however, conservation concerns about the destruction of the rain forests.

Precious and semiprecious stones, such as sapphires, rubies, topaz, and moonstones, are mined in Sri Lanka. The country also has hundreds of workshops where clothes are made for export.

Early settlers in Sri Lanka were the Sinhalese, who came from India in about 400 B.C. In the 1000s a second wave of immigrants arrived, the darker-skinned Tamils from southern India. The British ruled Sri Lanka from 1796. After independence in

1948 the Sinhalese, who are mainly Buddhist, took control. This caused resentment among the Tamils, who are mainly Hindu. In the 1980s a guerrilla army called the Tamil Tigers started a war of terrorism against the Sinhalese. The conflict continues today, effectively dividing the island in two. It has badly affected the blossoming tourist trade.

The Maldives

The Maldives is a set of coral islands lying 397 mi. (640km) to the southwest of Sri Lanka. Only 200 of the 1,200 islands are inhabited. Many are just tiny disks of white sand with clusters of coconut palms growing in the shallow soil.

None of the islands is more than 8 ft. (2.4m) above sea level, making the Maldives the world's flattest country. For this reason the local people are very concerned about rising sea levels. Some scientists have calculated that as a result of global warming, the sea may rise by as much as three feet (1m) by the year 2100. This would flood most of the islands. Pineapples, pomegranates, bananas, yams, and breadfruit (a huge tree

fruit that is cooked like a vegetable) grow on the islands. The Maldivians are good sailors, and they have a valuable fishing industry. Large catches of tuna and bonito are sold to Japan.

Increasing numbers of people make a living from the tourist trade. Many of the islands now have small luxury hotels on them. Guests arrive by boat and stay in beach houses.

Paradise island

The Maldives is an increasingly popular vacation destination. Tourists spend the days relaxing on the beaches or diving and snorkeling in the spectacular coral reefs.

AFGHANISTAN

Capital
Kabul
Area
249,700 sq. mi.
Population
26,813,057
Population density
107 per sq. mi.
Life expectancy
47 (m); 45 (f)
Religion
Islam
Languages
Pashto, Afghan Persian (Dari),
Turkic, and local languages
Adult literacy rate
31 percent
Currency
Afghani

 ARMENIA

Capital
Yerevan
Area
11,500 sq. mi.
Population
3,336,100
Population density
290 per sq. mi.
Life expectancy
62 (m); 71 (f)
Religion
Christianity
Language
Armenian
Adult literacy rate
99 percent
Currency
Dram

 **AZERBAIJAN**

Capital
Baku
Area
33,400 sq. mi.
Population
7,771,092
Population density
233 per sq. mi.
Life expectancy
59 (m); 67 (f)
Religions
Islam, Christianity
Language
Azerbaijani (Azeri)
Adult literacy rate
100 percent
Currency
Manat

 BAHRAIN

Capital
Manama
Area
240 sq. mi.
Population
645,361
Population density
2,704 per sq. mi.
Life expectancy
71 (m); 76 (f)
Religion
Islam
Languages
Arabic, English, Farsi, Urdu
Adult literacy rate
85 percent
Currency
Bahraini dinar

 BANGLADESH

Capital
Dhaka
Area
51,600 sq. mi.
Population
131,269,860
Population density
2,542 per sq. mi.
Life expectancy
61 (m); 60 (f)
Religions
Islam, Hinduism
Languages
Bengali, Bihari, and tribal
languages
Adult literacy rate
38 percent
Currency
Taka

 BHUTAN

Capital
Thimphu
Area
18,100 sq. mi.
Population
2,049,412
Population density
113 per sq. mi.
Life expectancy
53 (m); 52 (f)
Religions
Buddhism, Hinduism
Languages
Dzongkha, Tobetan, and
Nepalese dialects
Adult literacy rate
42 percent
Currency
Ngultrum

CYPRUS

Capital
Nicosia
Area
3,600 sq. mi.
Population
762,887
Population density
214 per sq. mi.
Life expectancy
75 (m); 79 (f)
Religions
Christianity, Islam
Languages
Greek, Turkish, English
Adult literacy rate
95 percent
Currency
Cyprian pound

 GEORGIA

Capital
Tbilisi
Area
26,900 sq. mi.
Population
4,989,285
Population density
186 per sq. mi.
Life expectancy
61 (m); 68 (f)
Religions
Christianity, Islam
Language
Georgian, Russian
Adult literacy rate
99 percent
Currency
Lavi

 INDIA

Capital
New Delhi
Area
1,146,600 sq. mi.
Population
1,029,991,145
Population density
898 per sq. mi.
Life expectancy
62 (m); 64 (f)
Religions
Hinduism, Islam,
Christianity, Sikhism
Languages
Hindi, English, and local
languages
Adult literacy rate
52 percent
Currency
Indian rupee

 IRAN

Capital
Tehran
Area
630,900 sq. mi.
Population
66,128,965
Population density
105 per sq. mi.
Life expectancy
69 (m); 71 (f)
Religion
Islam
Languages
Persian (Farsi), Turkic,
Kurdish, Luri
Adult literacy rate
72 percent
Currency
Iranian rial

 IRAQ

Capital
Baghdad
Area
167,400 sq. mi.
Population
23,331,985
Population density
139 per sq. mi.
Life expectancy
66 (m); 68 (f)
Religion
Islam
Languages
Arabic, Kurdish
Adult literacy rate
58 percent
Currency
Iraqi dinar

 ISRAEL

Capital
Jerusalem
Area
7,800 sq. mi.
Population
5,938,093
Population density
757 per sq. mi.
Life expectancy
77 (m); 81 (f)
Religions
Judaism, Islam, Christianity
Languages
Hebrew, Russian, Arabic,
English
Adult literacy rate
96 percent
Currency
New shekel

JORDAN

Capital
Amman
Area
35,300 sq. mi.
Population
5,153,378
Population density
146 per sq. mi.
Life expectancy
75 (m); 80 (f)
Religions
Islam
Languages
Arabic, English
Adult literacy rate
87 percent
Currency
Jordanian dinar

 KAZAKHSTAN

Capital
Astana
Area
1,047,900 sq. mi.
Population
16,731,303
Population density
16 per sq. mi.
Life expectancy
58 (m); 69 (f)
Religions
Islam, Christianity
Languages
Kazakh, Russian
Adult literacy rate
98 percent
Currency
Tenge

 **KUWAIT**

Capital
Kuwait City
Area
6,800 sq. mi.
Population
2,041,961
Population density
297 per sq. mi.
Life expectancy
75 (m); 77 (f)
Religion
Islam
Languages
Arabic, English
Adult literacy rate
79 percent
Currency
Kuwaiti dinar

 KYRGYZSTAN

Capital
Bishkek
Area
76,600 sq. mi.
Population
4,753,003
Population density
62 per sq. mi.
Life expectancy
59 (m); 68 (f)
Religions
Islam, Christianity
Languages
Kyrgyz (Cyrillic script; Latin
script to be reintroduced),
Russian
Adult literacy rate
97 percent
Currency
Som

 LEBANON

Capital
Beirut
Area
3,900 sq. mi.
Population
3,627,774
Population density
92 per sq. mi.
Life expectancy
69 (m); 74 (f)
Religions
Islam, Christianity
Languages
Arabic, French, English,
Armenian
Adult literacy rate
92 percent
Currency
Lebanese pound

 MALDIVES

Capital
Malé
Area
100 sq. mi.
Population
310,764
Population density
3,108 per sq. mi.
Life expectancy
61 (m); 64 (f)
Religion
Islam
Languages
Maldivian Divehi (Sinhalese
dialect), English
Adult literacy rate
93 percent
Currency
Rufiyaa

NEPAL

Capital
Kathmandu
Area
52,800 sq. mi.
Population
25,284,463
Population density
479 per sq. mi.
Life expectancy
59 (m); 58 (f)
Religions
Hinduism, Buddhism, Islam
Languages
Nepali, Maithir, Bhojpuri
Adult literacy rate
27 percent
Currency
Nepalese rupee

 OMAN

Capital
Muscat
Area
81,900 sq. mi.
Population
2,622,198
Population density
32 per sq. mi.
Life expectancy
70 (m); 74 (f)
Religion
Islam
Language
Arabic
Adult literacy rate
59 percent
Currency
Omani rial

 PAKISTAN

Capital
Islamabad
Area
300,300 sq. mi.
Population
144,616,639
Population density
482 per sq. mi.
Life expectancy
61 (m); 62 (f)
Religion
Islam
Languages
Urdu, Punjabi, Pashto,
Sindhi, English
Adult literacy rate
38 percent
Currency
Pakistani rupee

 QATAR

Capital
Doha
Area
4,200 sq. mi.
Population
769,152
Population density
181 per sq. mi.
Life expectancy
70 (m); 75 (f)
Religion
Islam
Languages
Arabic, English
Adult literacy rate
79 percent
Currency
Qatari riyal

 SAUDI ARABIA

Capital
Riyadh
Area
829,000 sq. mi.
Population
22,757,092
Population density
27 per sq. mi.
Life expectancy
66 (m); 70 (f)
Religion
Islam
Language
Arabic
Adult literacy rate
63 percent
Currency
Saudi Arabian riyal

 SRI LANKA

Capital
Colombo
Area
25,000 sq. mi.
Population
19,408,635
Population density
777 per sq. mi.
Life expectancy
70 (m); 75 (f)
Religions
Buddhism, Hinduism,
Christianity, Islam
Languages
Sinhala, Tamil, English
Adult literacy rate
88 percent
Currency
Sri Lankan rupee

SYRIA

Capital
Damascus
Area
71,000 sq. mi.
Population
16,728,808
Population density
236 per sq. mi.
Life expectancy
68 (m); 70 (f)
Religions
Islam, Christianity
Languages
Arabic, Kurdish, Armenian
Adult literacy rate
79 percent
Currency
Syrian pound

 TAJIKISTAN

Capital
Dushanbe
Area
55,200 sq. mi.
Population
6,578,681
Population density
119 per sq. mi.
Life expectancy
61 (m); 67 (f)
Religion
Islam
Languages
Tajik (Cyrillic script), Russian
Adult literacy rate
100 percent
Currency
Tajik ruble

 **TURKEY**

Capital
Ankara
Area
297,200 sq. mi.
Population
66,493,970
Population density
224 per sq. mi.
Life expectancy
69 (m); 74 (f)
Religion
Islam
Languages
Turkish, Kurdish, Arabic
Adult literacy rate
82 percent
Currency
Turkish lira

 TURKMENISTAN

Capital
Ashgabat
Area
188,200 sq. mi.
Population
4,603,244
Population density
24 per sq. mi.
Life expectancy
57 (m); 65 (f)
Religions
Islam, Christianity
Language
Turkmen (Latin-based script), Russian, Uzbek
Adult literacy rate
100 percent
Currency
Manat

 **UNITED ARAB EMIRATES**

Capital
Abu Dhabi
Area
32,000 sq. mi.
Population
2,407,460
Population density
75 per sq. mi.
Life expectancy
72 (m); 77 (f)
Religions
Islam, Christianity, Hinduism
Languages
Arabic, English, Persian, Hindi, Urdu
Adult literacy rate
79 percent
Currency
U.A.E. dirham

 UZBEKISTAN

Capital
Tashkent
Area
172,500 sq. mi.
Population
25,155,064
Population density
146 per sq. mi.
Life expectancy
60 (m); 68(f)
Religions
Islam, Christianity
Languages
Uzbek, Russian
Adult literacy rate
97 percent
Currency
Som

 YEMEN

Capital
Sanaa
Area
203,600 sq. mi.
Population
18,078,035
Population density
89 per sq. mi.
Life expectancy
58 (m); 62 (f)
Religion
Islam
Language
Arabic
Adult literacy rate
43 percent
Currency
Yemeni rial

Eastern Asia
MONGOLIA

Great rolling grasslands dominate the landscape of Mongolia, a vast country that lies between Russia and China. The Altai Mountains tower in the west, and the Gobi Desert covers much of the south. Despite its size, Mongolia has a population of just 2.7 million. On average there is fewer than one person per square mile.

Mongolia is one of the highest countries in the world—on average it is 5,182 ft. (1,580m) above sea level. Its highest mountains are in the far west. The Altai Mountains are permanently snowcapped, but between the peaks are stark deserts where rain hardly ever falls. Although landlocked, the country has many lakes for water supplies and fishing. The south is dominated by the Gobi Desert. It looks barren, but it has enough grass to support scattered herds of sheep, goats, and camels. Much of the rest of Mongolia is grassland.

Practical clothing

A deel (long cloth gown) forms the basis of Mongolian clothing. Its long sleeves can be rolled down to keep the hands warm.

Nomadic life

Traditionally most Mongolian families lived as seminomadic herders, moving around the steppes with their herds of cattle, sheep, horses, and camels. The herders moved at least twice per year, seeking new grazing land for their animals. They lived in *gers* (large, round tents). Made of felt and supported on wooden slats, *gers* could be put up and taken down quickly. They were surprisingly spacious and comfortable, with room for beds and furniture. All *gers* had a similar layout. The door always faced south, there was a place of honor set aside for guests, and treasured possessions were kept at the rear. On the back wall was the family altar with Buddhist images and family photos. Along with their main *ger* Mongolians also erected smaller *gers* for storage purposes.

Today, however, most rural people live on large livestock farms. Few follow the nomadic way of life.

Portable television

A nomadic family gathers outside their ger (dwelling) in the Mongolian steppes to watch a portable television powered by an electric generator.

On the road

Most Mongolian roads are little more than dirt tracks. They are dusty in the hot summers, muddy after heavy rains, and frozen hard during the long, cold winters. Herders use two-humped Bactrian camels to carry their possessions from place to place. Horses are also very important to Mongolian nomads—but not just for transporation. Airak, the nation's most popular drink, is made from mare's milk that has been fermented for about three days to make it slightly fizzy. Mongolians live mainly on a diet of milk, cheese, and meat. They do not eat many vegetables because so little of the land is suitable for growing crops.

Festivals and culture

Children of herding families are taught at home until the age of eight, when they are sent to small boarding schools in the towns or in the capital, Ulan Bator. All Mongolians learn to ride horses at a young age. In the summer children take part in horse racing festivals such as the great Naadam festival in Ulan Bator. The festival also includes other popular Mongolian sports such as wrestling and archery.

In the capital most people live in apartment blocks and work in offices and factories. However, they still love rural life, and many keep a *ger* on the outskirts of the city. Listening to music is a favorite pastime. Mongolians sing traditional songs about love, adventure, and life on the steppes, accompanied by a two-stringed *morin khur*, which is played like a cello.

Young rider
Mongolian children learn to ride horses at a young age and enjoy taking part in horse racing festivals. This boy is competing in the annual Naadam Festival.

CHINA

One person in every five in the world is Chinese. With over one billion citizens, the country has the largest population of any nation on earth. China covers a huge area of eastern Asia, but most of the people live in the eastern part of the country, where the river valleys and plains are good for farming and where most of the big industrial cities are clustered.

Workshop of the world

For many years the Communist Chinese government had control and ownership of all industries and food production. During this time China virtually cut itself off from the outside world.

Since the 1980s the government has given greater freedom to people to develop businesses for themselves and encouraged more international trade. Now China is booming. Cities of high-rise office blocks are being built, drawing in millions of workers from the country. Shenzhen, for example, was a small market town just 20 years ago, and now it has a population of over three million. The economic development of the past 20 years is mostly concentrated in Special Economic Zones in eastern China where foreigners have set up joint enterprises with the Chinese. Factories in these areas now produce a full range of goods from clothes to computer chips.

New ways

China has become less cut off from the rest of the world, and most cities now have fast-food restaurants selling American-style burgers.

Boom town

Shenzhen has grown rapidly in recent years. Its economic boom is mainly because of its location. It is near Hong Kong, an old British colony and a world financial center.

Old ways, new world

Traditional ways of life survive alongside modern developments, even in the big cities, such as Shanghai, Guangzhou (Canton), and Hong Kong. Pedal-power trishaw taxis gather in the squares, waiting for customers, and the street markets are packed with spices, fish, and fresh vegetables. Stalls sell snacks—dishes of rice and noodles eaten with chopsticks—freshly cooked in woks.

Chinese herbal medicines and the ancient art of acupuncture (inserting sharp needles into specific parts of the body) are used alongside Western medicine. Many stay healthy by practicing old martial arts, such as t'ai chi ch'uan, in the public squares.

Table tennis is still one of China's most popular sports. Traditional entertainments, such as the circus with its spectacularly skilled acrobats and the opera with its colorful tales of myth and legend retold through songs and dance, are always well attended. The Chinese New Year is celebrated with feasts, firecrackers, and displays by dancing dragon puppets.

Communist control

The dramatic economic changes in China have not been matched by political reform. The government still remains a one-party Communist state, exerting control over many aspects of people's lives. The media is not allowed to criticize the government, and political opponents can be imprisoned. This was made clear to the world in 1989, when the army crushed a peaceful revolt in Tiananmen Square, Beijing, led by students demanding greater freedom and democracy.

Feeding and looking after the huge population is China's most pressing task. For many years the government has attempted to slow population growth by encouraging families to have only one child. All one-child families are rewarded with priority housing and medical care.

Agriculture

Children in farming villages often help their parents in the fields. Many Chinese farmers still use labour-intensive, hand- or ox-powered equipment.

The many faces of China

Despite the rapid growth of cities, two thirds of China's population still lives in the country. Most farming villages have few of the high-tech gadgets and comforts of the new cities. Simple, one-story homes have just two rooms under a tiled roof. Pigs and chickens live in the muddy pens outside. The fields are often worked by ox-drawn plows and handheld shovels.

Ways of life differ with the climate and landscape. In Manchuria (Dongbei) in the far northeast the winters are bitterly cold, but the summers are long enough to grow good harvests of wheat, soya beans, sugar beets, sunflowers, and cotton. The Manchurian forests produce much of the timber used in China's industry, and the area is rich in minerals, notably coal and oil.

In the far west people live in and around the cities that once stood on the ancient overland trade routes called the Silk Road. They include nomadic Kazakh herders, who live in yurts (felt tents), and Persian-speaking Tajiks.

China is the world's leading producer of rice, most of which is produced in the warm and humid region to the south of the great Chang Jiang (Yangtze River), which runs through the middle of the country.

In the southwest lies Xizang (Tibet). Chinese rule over this Buddhist land set high in the Himalayas is a source of conflict. Many Tibetans want independence from China and the return of their spiritual leader, the Dalai Lama, who lives in exile.

Novice monks

Boys as young as eight are sent to Buddhist monasteries in Tibet to train as monks. They are allowed few possessions and spend much of their time meditating.

Food also varies from region to region. Specialities of the southeastern region include the fried noodle dish *châo mien* (chow mein), and dim sum (dumplings steamed in bamboo baskets). In Tibet the main food is *tsampa* (flat bread made with barley flour) eaten with a souplike tea flavored with yak butter.

Ancient wonders

Some 90 percent of the Chinese people belong to the Han ethnic group, but there are 55 official minority ethnic groups, each with its own customs and language.

Mandarin is the official language of China, but there are many other Chinese languages, such as Wu and Cantonese. The Chinese written language is not based on sounds but on pictures, which have evolved into characters. This means that written Chinese can be read by most Chinese speakers, regardless of the form of Chinese that they speak—they see the same character, understand its meaning, but pronounce it differently.

Calligraphy—the art of writing beautiful Chinese characters using a brush and ink—often forms part of paintings on sheets of paper or silk.

Street painting
An audience of Chinese schoolchildren watches an artist produce a giant-sized painting using a big brush and a bucket of ink.

Extraordinarily delicate and skilled paintings many hundreds of years old are evidence of China's history as one of the world's oldest and most sophisticated civilizations. It was ruled over by emperors for more than 2,000 years. Tourists from all over the world come to see the remains of this civilization. The Great Wall of China and the clay army—buried at Xi'an in 210 B.C.—are popular attractions. Once the emperors' grand Forbidden City, at the heart of Beijing, was out-of-bounds to everyone who was not a noble, but now it is open for all to explore and admire.

TAIWAN

Lying 100 miles off the coast of southeast China, the large island of Taiwan is a prosperous, industrialized nation. Much of the population come from mainland China originally, having fled Communist rule. A high ridge of forest-cloaked mountains lines the eastern coast, but most people live in the broad, fertile plains that stretch out to the west coast.

When Communists won control of China in 1949 following a bloody civil war, around two million defeated nationalists fled to Taiwan. They set up an alternative government, claiming to be the true Republic of China, and they waited for the opportunity to return to the mainland. This has never happened. China has repeatedly threatened to take over Taiwan, but the Taiwanese have support from the U.S.

Taiwan became a fast-growing industrial nation, producing clothes and electrical goods. It also became a leading producer of large-scale industrial products such as petrochemicals, ships, and aircraft, as well as high-tech goods such as computers and silicon chips.

Farms produce rice, sweet potatoes, and other vegetables, but frequently the plains are shrouded in smog from the thousands of factories—especially around Taipei, the capital city, where one third of the population lives.

There are about 200,000 original Taiwanese inhabitants, but 85 percent of the people originally came from China. They speak Mandarin, eat Chinese food, and practice Buddhism. They have also adopted American and Japanese pastimes such as golf and karaoke.

Dragon boats

Every year a Dragon Boat Festival takes place in Taiwan's capital, Taipei. Competing teams row their dragon-shaped boats to the beat of a drum.

JAPAN

Lying off of Asia's east coast, Japan is one of the world's leading industrial nations, famous for producing high-tech electronic goods. It is governed by a democratically elected parliament, called the Diet, and the current head of state is Emperor Akihito. The four main islands are connected by some of the world's biggest and most technical bridges and tunnels.

Industrial power

Japanese society is built on very solid foundations and cultural traditions. They believe strongly in loyalty, and people tend to work for the same employer for the whole of their lives. Many of the world's most familiar product names are Japanese, such as Nissan and Sony.

For many years it seemed that the rise of Japan's wealth was unstoppable as Japanese companies expanded worldwide. However, in the late 1990s the world economy began to shrink, and Japan's fortunes suddenly began to decline.

Modern city

Much of Japan's capital, Tokyo, was destroyed by bombs in World War II. Today it is a city of high-rise office blocks and sprawling suburbs.

The spirit world

Most people in Japan believe in a mixture of Shinto and Buddhism. Many festivals revolve around Shinto. They include harvest festivals and the Oshogatsu (New Year) Festival, when people go to a shrine and find out their prospects from pieces of paper with their fortunes printed on them.

Girls have their own Shinto festival day, Ohinamatsuri, when parents display dolls in honor of their daughters. For the boys' festival, Tango-no-Sekku, thousands of streamers shaped like carp are hung in the streets. In November at Shichi-go-san (seven-five-three) seven-year-old girls, boys of five, and girls and boys of three go to shrines in their finest traditional costumes to be blessed. On special occasions Japanese girls put on a kimono (a traditional silk robe that is decorated with intricate patterns and pictures).

Shinto, which means "the way of the gods," is a celebration of life and nature and involves the worship of the *kammi* (spirits) that are the creative forces in nature. Shrines are dedicated to a specific *kami* and are often found in places of spectacular natural beauty. Origami (the art of folding sheets of paper into shapes) is often used to decorate Shinto shrines.

Nature plays an important part in Japanese religion. Every spring millions go cherry-blossom viewing, and the gardens of the Zen Buddhists combine elements such as raked gravel and large rocks.

Festivals

Girls wear traditional, colorful kimonos (robes) when visiting Shinto temples for religious festivals.

Raw fish and seaweed

The Japanese eat dishes of fresh vegetables with meat or seafood. Rice is the main accompaniment. Yakitori (skewers of grilled chicken) is a popular kind of Japanese fast food, often bought from street vendors. Tempura is deep-fried seafood or vegetables coated in a light batter. Sushi consists of bite-sized rice bundles flavored with vegetables and wrapped in thin sheets of seaweed or topped with slices of raw fish.

The Japanese are the world's biggest fish eaters, and their large and modern fishing fleets take ten percent of the world's catch. Japan produces almost all of its own food. This is a remarkable feat, given that less than 20 percent of the land is suitable for agriculture. Most of Japan is covered by high mountains, and virtually all of the cities are on—or close to—the coast. This includes the capital, Tokyo, which has grown and merged with Yokohama to form the world's largest city, with over 27 million people. But there are still hundreds of old villages in rural areas, with clusters of ancient wooden houses under thatched or tiled roofs.

The strength of tradition

The cities are busy with traffic, neon signs, offices, stores, food stalls, discos, and bars. Many of the buildings are modern—although they tend to be low rather than high because Japan suffers regularly from earthquakes. A massive earthquake hit the city of Kobe, on Honshu Island, in 1995, killing more than 5,000 people and injuring 26,000 more. Small, harmless earth tremors are recorded every day.

Fish lunch
These Japanese schoolchildren are enjoying a packed lunch of sushi. They eat the fish and rice bundles using chopsticks.

Old traditions survive among the modern buildings. Houses and apartments have sliding screens made of paper, which separate the rooms. Apartment owners make tiny Zen gardens on their balconies, using bonzai (miniature) trees. They may sleep on tatami floor mats. Some larger homes still have a teahouse in the garden where the 500-year-old *cha-no-yu* (tea ceremony) can be performed, using carefully chosen pottery to serve whisked and frothy green tea.

Traditional music and theater are also popular. Gagaku (the ancient court music of Japan) is played by an ensemble of Japanese wind, string, and percussion instruments. In No plays performers wear masks and act and dance, while Bunraku theater brings puppets to life.

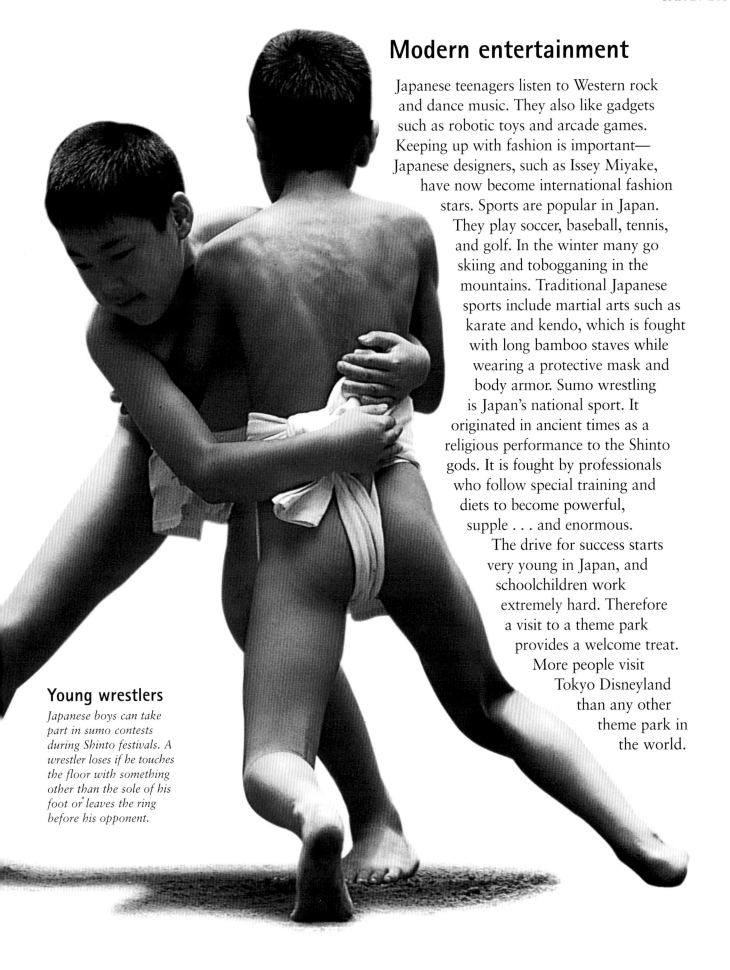

Modern entertainment

Japanese teenagers listen to Western rock and dance music. They also like gadgets such as robotic toys and arcade games. Keeping up with fashion is important—Japanese designers, such as Issey Miyake, have now become international fashion stars. Sports are popular in Japan. They play soccer, baseball, tennis, and golf. In the winter many go skiing and tobogganing in the mountains. Traditional Japanese sports include martial arts such as karate and kendo, which is fought with long bamboo staves while wearing a protective mask and body armor. Sumo wrestling is Japan's national sport. It originated in ancient times as a religious performance to the Shinto gods. It is fought by professionals who follow special training and diets to become powerful, supple . . . and enormous.

The drive for success starts very young in Japan, and schoolchildren work extremely hard. Therefore a visit to a theme park provides a welcome treat. More people visit Tokyo Disneyland than any other theme park in the world.

Young wrestlers

Japanese boys can take part in sumo contests during Shinto festivals. A wrestler loses if he touches the floor with something other than the sole of his foot or leaves the ring before his opponent.

KOREA

The broad peninsula of Korea sticks out like a thumb from China toward Japan. The landscape ranges from high mountains and forests to fertile plains. The summers are warm and sunny, but the winters are very cold. In the fall the leaves of the gingko, poplar, and maple trees blaze with yellow, red, and gold.

Divided nation

In the early decades of the 1900s Korea was ruled by Japan. However, after the Japanese left at the end of World War II the country was split in two. In 1948 a Communist government under Kim Il Sung took over in North Korea, and in 1950 North Korea invaded South Korea. The Korean War (1950–53) pitched the North (supported by China) against the South (supported by the United Nations). The peace treaty called for the peninsula to be divided in two once again.

The two halves of Korea are very different. North Korea is Communist. The people work on government-owned farms, in the mines producing coal, iron, and copper, and in factories. Isolated from the rest of the world, the North Koreans remain poor. In contrast South Korea has become one of the region's leading industrial nations. Many families were split up by the division of Korea. For years North Korea refused any contact with the South, but it now allows limited exchange visits.

Land of traditions

Korea has a distinct language with its own alphabet, called Hangul, based entirely on sounds.

Entertainment

Folk songs are popular in both North and South Korea. These North Korean children are playing accordions.

Mountain land

Korea is a mountainous country, but the mountain areas are largely uninhabited.

The peninsula also has its own types of food. *Bulgogi* is sometimes called "Korean barbecue." Strips of meat are cooked at the table on a dome-shaped hot plate. *Shin sul ro* is a meat stew with vegetables and nuts and is popular as a warm winter dish. Some Koreans still eat dishes made of dog and snake. But most famous of all is the Korean speciality called kimchi, a kind of pickle that accompanies most meals. In the fall groups of families and friends gather to make large quantities of winter kimchi. Cabbage and white radish are chopped up, mixed with red chili peppers, onion, garlic, and salt, and then placed in large pottery jars, which are then buried in the garden or placed on a cool balcony to ferment.

Buddhism and Christianity are the dominant religions in South Korea. There is also a Korean religion called Chondogyo, which combines Christianity, Buddhism, Chinese philosophies, and ancient beliefs. Beautiful, multistoried pagoda temples and statues of Buddha are located throughout Korea.

SOUTHEAST ASIA

The countries of Southeast Asia occupy a large chunk of hilly mainland, a long, thin peninsula, and thousands of islands. There are more than 13,000 islands in Indonesia and about 7,000 in the Philippines. Plants grow well in the warm climate, watered by frequent rains and heavy downpours during the rainy season, which lasts almost half the year.

Many of the hilly areas are covered in tropical forests. Elsewhere, steplike terraces have been cut into hillsides to grow rice in flooded fields, quilting the landscape with patches of vivid emerald-green. Mighty rivers, such as the Mekong and Irrawaddy, thread through the larger landmasses and serve as transportation routes for riverboats carrying passengers and goods to towns far inland.

The hot climate has a strong influence on the way people live. The traditional dress in many of these countries is a sarong (a simple, wraparound skirt). Made of a broad strip of printed cotton cloth, it may be worn by both

Stilt house

This home in northern Vietnam has been built on stilts so that it will not be flooded during the heavy rains of the annual monsoon (rainy) season.

men and women. Houses often have shutters instead of glass windows because they allow the air to circulate. Village houses are often raised above the ground on stilts so they are not flooded in very heavy rains.

In Bangkok, the capital of Thailand, an area called the Klongs is permanently flooded by the Chao Phraya River—so all the houses are built on very long stilts. The canals between the houses serve as streets, and the only way to travel around is by boat. Floating stores bring fresh vegetables and household goods.

Headmen and presidents

For most people in Southeast Asia the village is the most important center of activity. Even large cities in Indonesia and Malaysia have kampongs (villagelike areas). Traditionally the villages are made up of family groups, or clans, ruled by a headman and his council. Village leaders will try to get everyone to agree before

any vital decision is made, a process known as reaching a consensus. The national governments of Southeast Asia try to govern in a similar way.

Most of the countries are democracies, but the true power of the people to change their governments varies. Voters have no power in Myanmar (Burma), which has a military government. Laos and Vietnam are communist countries, which have only one party from which to choose. The heads of state are usually presidents or prime ministers, but Thailand, Cambodia, and Malaysia have kings or princes, and Brunei is ruled by a sultan.

Village life

This Vietnamese boy is bringing harvested rice back to his village. Vietnam is the fourth largest producer of rice in the world.

Asian tigers

During the last few decades of the 1900s some countries in Southeast Asia went through a period of rapid change. They began to develop new industries, and they built factories to make cars, televisions, computer equipment, and clothes. The more successful of these countries—Singapore, Thailand, Indonesia, Malaysia, and the Philippines—formed a powerful trading group called the Association of Southeast Asian Nations (ASEAN) and were nicknamed "Asian tigers."

In 1997, however, the world economy went into decline, causing great difficulties for these countries. Nonetheless, the ASEAN countries are still the leading industrial nations of the region. Malaysia has rich resources in tin, oil, rubber, and timber. Indonesia has copper, oil, and gas. Tiny Brunei, which joined ASEAN in 1984, is one of the world's leading oil producers.

As a result of the boom years, the cities of Southeast Asia have also grown fast. The centers of the biggest cities, such as Indonesia's capital, Jakarta, are very modern, with air-conditioned office blocks and elegant shopping malls. Malaysia's capital, Kuala Lumpur, has the world's tallest building, the Petronas Twin Towers, completed in 1997 and rising to 1,482 ft. (452m) with 88 floors.

Many people have moved to the cities from the country in hope of finding work. Thousands live in poor shanty towns that cluster around the outskirts of cities, including Jakarta and the Philippine capital, Manila.

Mango farming

Most people in Southeast Asia still live in rural areas, making a living by farming—producing rice and a wide range of vegetables and other crops such as mangoes, coconuts, and sugarcane. Many people make a living from the sea, catching fish from trawlers or traditional outrigger sailing canoes carved from tree trunks. These food products may be exported or go to factories specializing in food processing. But many also end up at the lively street markets, full of color, noise, and strong smells.

High rise

The 88-story Petronas Twin Towers in Malaysia's capital, Kuala Lumpur, were completed in 1997. They are made of glass, steel, and concrete. The two towers are joined at the 41st and 42nd floors (574 ft./175m above street level) by a 192-ft. (58.4-m) skybridge.

Rice harvest

More than one fifth of the world's rice is grown in Southeast Asia. The rice is grown on flooded terraces cut into the hillsides. Much of it is still harvested by hand, which is backbreaking work for the farming communities.

A mosaic of religions

In the past most people in Southeast Asia followed traditional religions, focusing on nature spirits and the spirits of their ancestors. In Thailand almost every family and business still has a miniature "spirit house," where daily devotions are made to the guardian spirits.

Southeast Asia has a long history as a center for trade—foreign merchants brought not only goods but ideas. About 2,000 years ago Indian traders brought Hinduism to the region. Later, traders and missionaries brought Buddhism, and several powerful empires adopted a mixture of the two called Hindu-Buddhism. Huge temples were built at Angkor Wat in Cambodia and Borobudur in Indonesia.

Around 1250 traders from India brought Islam, and it spread throughout many of the islands and into Malaysia. Today, Indonesia has more Muslims than any other country in the world. The small Indonesian island of Bali, however, is predominantly Hindu. Every village has three temples, so there is a total of about 20,000 temples on the island.

The Spanish brought Christianity to the Philippines, and 87 percent of the population belong to the Roman Catholic Church. Thailand, Myanmar, and

Religious mix

These temple goers are Caodaists. Caodaism has several million followers in Vietnam. It combines elements from many of the world's religions.

Faith schooling

Most people in Indonesia follow Islam, and children study the Koran (the holy book of the Muslim world) at school. They learn to recite complex passages from memory.

Hindu offering

This young woman carries an offering to a Hindu temple in Bali. Worship in the temple is led by a priest called a brahman.

Laos are mainly Buddhist. Orange-robed Buddhist monks can be seen in the numerous temples or collecting food offerings in the street from members of the public. In Thailand many men at some point in their lives take a few months off work to become temporary monks.

Religion is usually the main focus of the many traditional festivals. Loy Krathong is a Thai Festival that takes place during the full moon in November. People float candles on little banana-leaf boats on rivers, ponds, and canals in the hope that their prayers will be answered. In the Hindu Thaipusam festival celebrated in Singapore and Malaysia devotees painlessly pierce their bodies with skewers and hooks.

Importance of education

Education is a high priority in all Southeast
Asian countries. Most nations in the region have
a high literacy (the number of people who can
read and write) rate. In small country villages,
and even in the shantytowns that rim the big
cities, children go to school every day.

In Bali children are so highly regarded that
their feet are not allowed to touch the ground
for the first year of their lives, and there are
special ceremonies to mark every stage of
their lives. But not all children in Southeast
Asia are so lucky. In the big cities they are
frequently sent out to work, perhaps selling
newspapers or cigarettes at traffic lights.
Some even sift through the garbage dumps,
going through piles of stinking garbage in
search of anything that can be recycled.

Layers of language

The ancestors of the modern population of
Southeast Asia originally came from southern
China about 5,000 years ago. They brought
with them their own languages such as
Malay, Thai, Khmer (Cambodian),
Vietnamese, and Pilipino. But
there are many other local
languages. Myanmar (Burma),
for example, has at least 100
languages other than Burmese.

In Malaysia and Indonesia traders developed
a kind of market language called Bahasa. Today,
Bahasa Malaysian and Bahasa Indonesian are
the official languages of these countries.

In 1511 the first Europeans arrived
in Southeast Asia in search of the
precious spices of the "Spice

Good results

*Although Vietnam is a poor
country with a troubled past,
it has a high literacy rate.
Because education is so
important, students have
to do a lot of homework.*

Islands," a group of Indonesian islands called the Moluccas where nutmeg and cloves grow. Soon after, the Dutch, English, and Spanish began to take over parts of Southeast Asia, and by the end of the 1800s Thailand was the only country not ruled by a European nation. The British ruled Burma, Malaysia, and Singapore; the French ruled Cambodia, Laos, and Vietnam; the Dutch ruled Indonesia; and the Spanish (and later the U.S.) ruled the Philippines. The British brought large numbers of Chinese and Indian workers to Malaysia and Singapore, and many of their descendants still live there.

All of these countries became independent in the second half of the 1900s, but they retain reminders of this past, seen in government buildings and in the rubber and tea plantations. Malaysia, Singapore, and Brunei still belong to the British Commonwealth.

Exercise yard

These Vietnamese children are having a gym class in their schoolyard. As well as reading and writing, they are taught math, science, foreign languages, and Vietnamese history. The literacy rate in Vietnam is 93%.

Troubled lands

After Vietnam gained independence from France in 1954 the country was divided in half, with Communist control of the north. War broke out between the north and south. The U.S. supported South Vietnam and became deeply involved in the conflict. By the time South Vietnam surrendered in 1975, the war had cost the lives of more than 1.5 million Vietnamese and 60,000 Americans.

Cambodia was cast into turmoil when the Khmer Rouge regime, led by Pol Pot, ruled the country from 1975 to 1979. More than two million people (almost one third of the country's total population) were executed or died of famine during this time.

On parade

Well-dressed in their school uniforms, these Vietnamese girls are visiting the tomb of Communist leader Ho Chi Minh on the date of his birthday, which is a national holiday.

Sporting nations

Soccer is played throughout Southeast Asia. Badminton is a big sport in Indonesia, and baseball is popular in the Philippines. There are also more traditional sports and games. *Takraw* (or *chin-lon*) is similar to soccer and is played with a rattan (cane) ball. Thai boxing, in which kicking is allowed, is practiced in Thailand. Competitive kite flying takes place throughout Thailand, Malaysia, and Indonesia. In some kite-flying events contestants stick powdered glass to the line to try to saw through the lines of rival kite flyers.

Puppets, dancing, and arts

When Hinduism arrived in Southeast Asia, it was adopted first by the royal courts. As in India, temple ceremonies were accompanied by elaborate dances designed to please the gods. Complex and ornate forms of dancing developed, especially in Thailand and in Indonesia, and these traditions continue to this day. In Indonesia gamelan orchestras, made up almost entirely of xylophones, accompany the dancers.

Shadow puppets were used to illustrate tales from the great Hindu epics, and puppetry remains a popular form of entertainment both in Indonesia and Malaysia. With just a flaming oil lamp, a screen made from a sheet of white material, and a box full of silhouette puppets cut from leather, skilled puppeteers can hold an audience spellbound with love stories, clowning, and giant battle scenes, complete with flying arrows and lances.

There are hundreds of gifted

Temple dance
Colorfully dressed young dancers perform a graceful routine in Angkor Wat, a magnificent Hindu temple in Cambodia.

sculptors and painters across the region. They decorate the Buddhist temples of Thailand, the huge houses of the Toraja people on the Indonesian island of Sulawesi, and carve masks, fruits, animals, and statues of the gods in Bali.

In the Philippines the jeepneys (jeeplike taxis) are decorated from top to bottom, inside and out, with paintings, stickers, sculptures, lights, and tassels.

Tourism is an important source of income in Southeast Asia. The region can offer everything from luxury beach resorts to hikes in the remote rain forests of Borneo. Indonesia alone receives over 4.5 million tourists every year.

BRUNEI

Capital
Bandar Seri Begawan
Area
2,000 sq. mi.
Population
343,653
Population density
169 per sq. mi.
Life expectancy
71 (m); 76 (f)
Religions
Islam, Buddhism, Christianity
Languages
Malay, Chinese, English
Adult literacy rate
88 per cent
Currency
Brunei Dollar

 CAMBODIA

Capital
Phnom Penh
Area
68,100 sq. mi.
Population
12,491,501
Population density
184 per sq. mi.
Life expectancy
55 (m); 59 (f)
Religion
Buddhism
Languages
Khmer, French
Adult literacy rate
65 percent
Currency
Riel

 CHINA

Capital
Beijing
Area
3,596,600 sq. mi.
Population
1,273,111,290
Population density
354 per sq. mi.
Life expectancy
70 (m); 74 (f)
Religions
Taoism, Buddhism,
Christianity, Islam
Languages
Mandarin, Yue (Cantonese),
Wu, Hakka, Xiang, Gan,
Minbei, Minnan, and others
Adult literacy rate
82 percent
Currency
Renminbi (Yuan)

Population control

China's population was growing so fast that the communist government introduced a policy of penalizing families who had more than one child. This law has been relaxed in recent years.

Rocky grave

This graveyard in Indonesia is carved into the rock face. Balconies of tau tau *(small wooden statues representing grave guardians) stand watch.*

 EAST TIMOR

Capital
Dili
Area
5,641 sq. mi.
Population
920,000
Population density
163 per sq. mi.
Life expectancy
49 (m); 50 (f)
Religions
Islam, Christianity
Languages
Bahasa Indonesian, Portuguese, Timor, Tetun, and other local languages
Adult Literacy Rate
Unknown
Currency
U.S. dollar

 INDONESIA

Capital
Jakarta
Area
704,400 sq. mi.
Population
228,437,870
Population density
324 per sq. mi.
Life expectancy
66 (m); 71 (f)
Religions
Islam, Christianity
Languages
Bahasa Indonesian, English, Dutch, Javanese
Adult literacy rate
84 percent
Currency
Rupiah

 **JAPAN**

Capital
Tokyo
Area
152,200 sq. mi.
Population
126,771,662
Population density
867 per sq. mi.
Life expectancy
77 (m); 84 (f)
Religions
Shintoism, Buddhism
Language
Japanese
Adult literacy rate
100 percent
Currency
Yen

LAOS

Capital
Vientiane
Area
89,000 sq. mi.
Population
5,635,967
Population density
63 per sq. mi.
Life expectancy
52 (m); 55 (f)
Religions
Buddhism, traditional beliefs
Languages
Lao, French, English
Adult literacy rate
57 percent
Currency
Kip

 **MALAYSIA**

Capital
Kuala Lumpur
Area
126,700 sq. mi.
Population
22,229,040
Population density
175 per sq. mi.
Life expectancy
69 (m); 74 (f)
Religions
Islam, Buddhism, Hinduism,
Christianity
Languages
Malay, English, Chinese
dialects
Adult literacy rate
83 percent
Currency
Ringgit

 **MONGOLIA**

Capital
Ulan Bator
Area
603,500 sq. mi.
Population
2,654,999
Population density
4 per sq. mi.
Life expectancy
62 (m); 67 (f)
Religion
Buddhism
Language
Khalkha Mongol
Adult literacy rate
83 percent
Currency
Tugrik

Tent life

Outside of the big towns and cities many nomadic
Mongolians chose to live in traditional gers (tents).

MYANMAR

Capital
Yangon (Rangoon)
Area
262,000 sq. mi.
Population
41,734,853
Population density
159 per sq. mi.
Life expectancy
54 (m); 57 (f)
Religions
Buddhism, Christianity, Islam
Language
Burmese
Adult literacy rate
83 percent
Currency
Kyat

NORTH KOREA

Capital
Pyongyang
Area
46,400 sq. mi.
Population
21,968,228
Population density
473 per sq. mi.
Life expectancy
68 (m); 74 (f)
Religions
Chondogyo (combines
elements of Roman
Catholicism, Buddhism,
Taoism, and Shamanism),
Confucianism, Buddhism
Language
Korean
Adult literacy rate
95 percent
Currency
North Korean won

PHILIPPINES

Capital
Manila
Area
115,000 sq. mi.
Population
82,841,518
Population density
720 per sq. mi.
Life expectancy
65 (m); 71 (f)
Religions
Christianity, Islam
Languages
Pilipino, English
Adult literacy rate
95 percent
Currency
Filipino peso

SINGAPORE

Capital
Singapore
Area
250 sq. mi.
Population
4,300,419
Population density
17,202 per sq. mi.
Life expectancy
77 (m); 83 (f)
Religions
Buddhism, Taoism, Islam,
Christianity, Hinduism
Languages Malay, Chinese
(Mandarin), Tamil, English
Adult literacy rate
91 percent
Currency
Singaporean dollar

SOUTH KOREA

Capital
Seoul
Area
37,900 sq. mi.
Population
47,904,370
Population density
1,265 per sq. mi.
Life expectancy
71 (m); 79 (f)
Religions
Christianity, Buddhism
Language
Korean
Adult literacy rate
98 percent
Currency
South Korean won

 TAIWAN

Capital
Taipei
Area
12,400 sq. mi.
Population
22,370,461
Population density
1,798 per sq. mi.
Life expectancy
74 (m); 80 (f)
Religions
Buddhism, Taoism,
Confucianism, Christianity
Languages
Chinese (Mandarin), Taiwanese
Adult literacy rate
94 percent
Currency
New Taiwan dollar

 THAILAND

Capital
Bangkok
Area
197,400 sq. mi.
Population
61,797,751
Population density
313 per sq. mi.
Life expectancy
66 (m); 72 (f)
Religions
Buddhism, Islam
Languages
Thai, English
Adult literacy rate
94 percent
Currency
Baht

Vietnam

The winters are cold in northern Vietnam, so this mother has dressed her young children in warm clothes.

 VIETNAM

Capital
Hanoi
Area
125,500 sq. mi.
Population
79,939,014
Population density
637 per sq. mi.
Life expectancy
67 (m); 72 (f)
Religions
Taoism, Buddhism,
Christianity, traditional beliefs
Languages
Vietnamese, French, Chinese
(Mandarin), English
Adult literacy rate
94 percent
Currency
Dong

Australia

New Zealand

Pacific Islands

AUSTRALIA AND THE PACIFIC

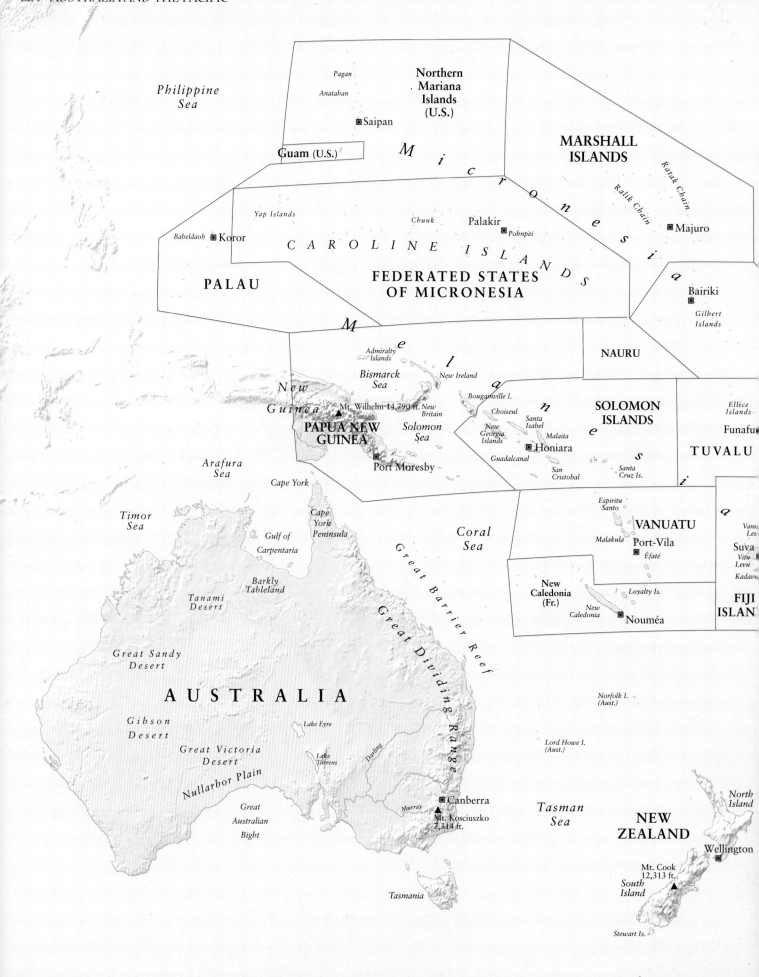

Philippine Sea

Pagan

Anatahan

Northern Mariana Islands (U.S.)

■ Saipan

Guam (U.S.)

M i c r o n e s i a

MARSHALL ISLANDS

Ratak Chain

Ralik Chain

Yap Islands

Chuuk

Palakir

■ *Pohnpei*

Majuro ■

Babeldaob ■ Koror

C A R O L I N E   I S L A N D S

PALAU

FEDERATED STATES OF MICRONESIA

a

M

■ Bairiki

Gilbert Islands

e

NAURU

Admiralty Islands

l

Bismarck Sea

New Ireland

New Britain

SOLOMON ISLANDS

Ellice Islands

Funafu

New Guinea

▲ Mt. Wilhelm 14,790 ft.

Bougainville I.

Choiseul

New Georgia Islands

Santa Isabel

Malaita

n

TUVALU

PAPUA NEW GUINEA

Solomon Sea

■ Honiara

e

Guadalcanal

San Cristobal

Santa Cruz Is.

s

■ Port Moresby

Arafura Sea

Cape York

i

Espiritu Santo

Coral Sea

VANUATU

Vanu Lev

Malakula

Port-Vila

■ *Éfaté*

Suva

Vitu Levu

a

Timor Sea

Cape York Peninsula

Gulf of Carpentaria

Barkly Tableland

Tanami Desert

Great Sandy Desert

New Caledonia (Fr.)

Loyalty Is.

Kadavu

FIJI ISLAN

New Caledonia

■ Nouméa

AUSTRALIA

Gibson Desert

Lake Eyre

Great Barrier Reef

Great Dividing Range

Norfolk I. (Aust.)

Great Victoria Desert

Lake Torrens

Darling

Lord Howe I. (Aust.)

Nullarbor Plain

Great Australian Bight

Murray

■ Canberra

▲ Mt. Kosciuszko 7,314 ft.

Tasman Sea

NEW ZEALAND

North Island

Wellington ■

Tasmania

Mt. Cook 12,313 ft. ▲

South Island

Stewart Is.

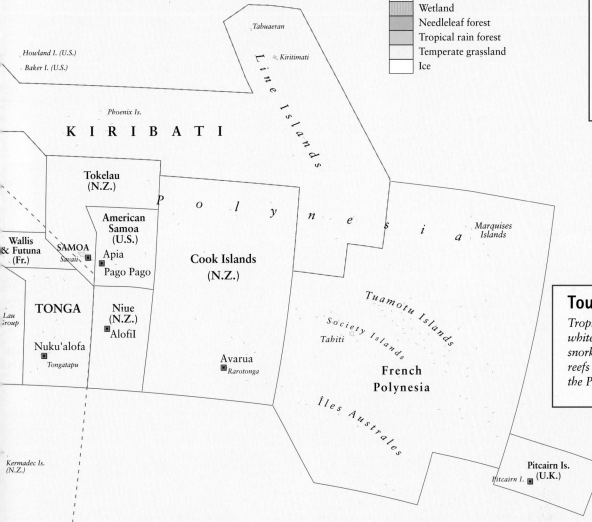

Hawaiian
Islands
(U.S.)

P A C I F I C

O C E A N

Mountain
Desert
Tundra
Cropland
Wetland
Needleleaf forest
Tropical rain forest
Temperate grassland
Ice

Palmyra (U.S.)

Tabuaeran

Kiritimati

Howland I. (U.S.)

Baker I. (U.S.)

Line Islands

Phoenix Is.

K I R I B A T I

Tokelau
(N.Z.)

P   o   l   y   n   e   s   i   a

American
Samoa
(U.S.)

Marquises
Islands

Wallis
& Futuna
(Fr.)

SAMOA

Apia

Savaii

Pago Pago

Cook Islands
(N.Z.)

Tuamotu Islands

Lau
Group

TONGA

Niue
(N.Z.)

AlofiI

Society Islands

Tahiti

Nuku'alofa

Tongatapu

Avarua

Rarotonga

French
Polynesia

Îles Australes

Pitcairn Is.
(U.K.)

Pitcairn I.

Kermadec Is.
(N.Z.)

P A C I F I C

O C E A N

International Date Line

Chatham Is.
(N.Z.)

0   1000   2000 km

0   500   1000 miles

N

City life

Over 85 percent of the Australian population lives in cities. The biggest city is Sydney, but the capital is Canberra.

Volcanic islands

Many of the Pacific Islands were formed when the tops of volcanoes pushed up from the seabed.

Tourist haven

Tropical climates, white-sand beaches, and snorkeling in the coral reefs attract tourists to the Pacific Islands.

Maori land

Maoris were the first settlers in New Zealand 1,200 years ago. Most of today's inhabitants are descended from British migrants.

AUSTRALIA

Australians sometimes refer to their homeland as "the lucky country." It has sunny weather most of the year, with fine beaches and warm blue seas. There is plenty of fertile land, a wealth of natural resources, and an energetic, resourceful population. Australians pride themselves on living well and enjoying life.

Australia is vast—the sixth largest country in the world—but very little of the land is inhabited. The population stands at just 19.4 million, which means that averaged out over the entire surface area of Australia there is fewer than one person for every square mile. Most people live close to the coast in the southeast. This is where three of the largest cities lie—Sydney, Melbourne, and Brisbane. Another large city, Perth, is 1,860 mi. (3,000km) away on the west coast. Much of what lies between the west coast and the east coast is desert—hot, dry plains of sand and gravel. The only town in the "red center" of Australia (so-called because of the color of the desert soil) is Alice Springs.

Red rocks

The impressive red mountains of the Olgas in the Australian outback are considered sacred by the Aboriginal people.

Flying farmers

In Australia's hot and humid north farmers grow sugarcane and tropical fruits. In the cooler south they grow wheat, potatoes, and the grapes that are used to make Australia's world-famous wines.

In the great belts of scrubland and bush in the remote "outback," which lies between the coastal regions and the desert, there are huge livestock farms where large flocks of sheep and herds of cattle are raised. A single sheep farm may cover 3,100 mi. (5,000km). These farms are so big that the farm workers sometimes use small aircraft to check their herds, and stockmen get around using motorbikes and quadbikes.

Families running the farms often live far from the nearest neighbors or towns. Because they are so far from any school, children are taught at home, with classes conducted by the School of the Air on two-way radios or over the Internet. If they become sick, the flying doctor arrives by plane.

Farming plays an important part in Australia's

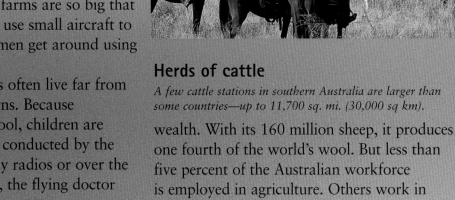

Herds of cattle
A few cattle stations in southern Australia are larger than some countries—up to 11,700 sq. mi. (30,000 sq km).

wealth. With its 160 million sheep, it produces one fourth of the world's wool. But less than five percent of the Australian workforce is employed in agriculture. Others work in manufacturing, car production, electrical goods, and textiles or in service industries such as banking and finance.

Who are the Australians?

When Captain Cook raised his flag at Botany Bay, just south of Sydney, in 1770 and claimed Australia for England, he knew very little about the people already living there. In fact there were around 600 native groups, with about 300 separate languages. They became known simply as the Aboriginals (from the Latin *ab origine*, "from the beginning"). Their ancestors had come to Australia at least 40,000 years earlier.

Each group had developed their own way of life according to their surroundings, which differed hugely from the tropical north to the cool mountains of the island of Tasmania in the far south. They lived by hunting and fishing, using spears, nets, and boomerangs, and by gathering edible plants, nuts, fruits, and insect grubs (such as the large and nutritious witchetty grubs). They traded goods, including stone tools, natural dyes, and precious shells, right across the continent. As a result, they developed an intimate knowledge of the land and its wildlife and built this into their religious beliefs and their myths and legends.

European settlers

This ancient pattern of life suddenly came under threat after Captain Cook's visit. In 1788 the British sent their first shipload of European settlers to Australia. At first these were criminals sent to Australia as a punishment—often for minor crimes such as poaching or picking pockets. In total, over 160,000 criminals were transported to Australia, and many stayed to make a living as farmers. Other European settlers also came to Australia, making new lives for themselves in the fertile lands and new cities.

The Aboriginal people were powerless to stop the Europeans. They had only primitive weapons and little resistance to the diseases that the Europeans brought with them such as measles. The Europeans took their land, introduced completely new ways of life, such as sheep farming, and many Aboriginal people were killed. The total number of Aboriginal people fell rapidly, from about 300,000 in the 1770s to just 70,000 in the 1930s.

Preserving traditions

Since that time, the Aboriginal people have been better treated, and their numbers have increased to 200,000—but this is only 1.5 percent of Australia's total population.

Aboriginal art

Aboriginal artists drew pictures in the sand, on trees, and, like this one, on rock surfaces. Traditionally they used brushes made from sticks that had been chewed until the ends were frayed.

The Aboriginal people are anxious to preserve their traditions such as the sacred rituals of music making, and body painting. Aboriginal people believe the land is a sacred place with unseen spiritual forces, and natural landmarks, such as mountains and trees, are treated as holy sites. They also keep stories alive about the "Dreamtime"—a distant time when they believe the landscape came into being. Their traditional dot paintings often depict the mythical Dreamtime creatures.

In recent decades the Aboriginal people have had some success in claiming back large tracts of their land from the Australian government, and they now control how this land is used.

An international land

The population of newer Australian settlers has changed significantly. Up until about 50 years ago most of them came from Europe, mainly from Great Britain and Ireland. After World War II a large number of immigrants came from Greece, Italy, and Turkey. More recently there has been an influx of immigrants from Asia.

As a result, Australia's cities are a melting pot of cultures. Immigrant communities have brought with them their own religions, festivals, and foods. Sydney, for example, is famous for its great range of restaurants, serving cuisine from all over the world.

New generation

Although many Aboriginal people still live in the outback, the majority now live in towns. Aboriginal people are very proud of their culture and traditions and pass them on to their children.

Sun, sand, and sports

More than 80 percent of Australians live in towns along the coast within easy reach of the beach. They make the most of their sunny climate—swimming, surfing, sailing, or simply enjoying a barbecue all year round. Possibly because of their outdoor lifestyle, the Australians are superb at sports. Just think of Shane Warne (cricket), Cathy Freeman (track and field), or Lleyton Hewitt (tennis).

Rules of the game

These boys are playing a type of football called Australian Rules. It is played with an oval ball on an oval field.

Wildlife wonders

Cut adrift from the rest of the world, Australia is home to some very unusual animals. Kangaroos, wombats, wallabies, and koalas are all marsupials (mammals with a pocket or pouch on their stomachs for carrying and nursing babies). The country's unique animal kingdom includes the platypus and the echidna, the only mammals that lay eggs. There are also some extremely dangerous creatures such as sharks, jellyfish, and the saltwater crocodile and some of the most poisonous snakes and spiders in the world.

King crab

Two children enjoy the beach in the company of a giant king crab, one of the world's largest crabs.

A people apart

Australia has strong links with Great Britain. The main language is English—although Australian English has distinctive touches with its own accent, words such as *tucker* (food), *dinkum* (genuine), and the greeting "G'day"(Good day). Most of the institutions, including the education and justice systems, are based on British models. Queen Elizabeth II is the head of state and is represented in Australia by the Governor-General. However, a growing number of Australians want their country to break free from its historic ties with Great Britain and to become a republic, headed by a president rather that the British monarch. In 1999 the Australians voted by a narrow majority to stay loyal to the queen.

Australia's outlook on the world is changing. Increasingly, as trade and cultural links develop with closer neighboring countries, such as Japan, China, and the Pacific Islands, Australians see themselves more as a part of the Pacific than a part of distant Europe—which, after all, lies on the other side of the globe.

Dramatic view

Sydney is Australia's financial and business center. The bridge and opera house in Sydney's harbor are very popular tourist attractions.

National identity

Although the Australian flag contains Great Britain's Union Jack, many in Australia believe it is time the country left behind its colonial roots.

NEW ZEALAND

Lying in the South Pacific Ocean, 992 mi. (1,596km) southeast of Australia, New Zealand is a land of snow-capped mountains and fiery volcanoes, of gurgling rivers and still lakes, deep forests and lush pasture, and dramatic, rocky coastlines. It is divided into two large islands, called the North Island and the South Island, and a smattering of smaller islands.

Kiwis

Agriculture is New Zealand's primary industry. Highly geared toward export markets, it uses modern and efficient farming methods. From herds of dairy cattle, farmers produce New Zealand's famous butter and cheese, and the sheep provide wool and meat. The well-watered pastures are able to support large herds, with high yields of milk, meat, and wool. New Zealand has a population of 3.8 million, but its sheep population is estimated to be 45 million.

Forestry is another important industry. Conifer trees are grown for timber, chipboard, and to make paper. Fishing for lobsters, crayfish, oysters, and numerous other kinds of seafood also provides valuable exports.

Sheep farming

New Zealand's lush pastures are perfect for sheep farming. Sheep were first brought to the country by Captain Cook in 1773.

In recent years New Zealand has become famous for another export—a fruit developed in the North Island from a Chinese berry that grows on thick vines. Once called a Chinese gooseberry, it is now better known as a kiwi fruit. "Kiwi" is also the name of a flightless bird that is unique to the country.

City life

Only 15 percent of New Zealanders live in the country. The rest live in the towns and cities. The biggest city is Auckland in the north of the North Island. It is also the country's main port. The capital, Wellington, is in the south of the North Island. High-rise offices front the harbor in the financial and administrative center, but the windy and earthquake-prone hillsides behind are dotted with timber houses.

Although larger, the colder, more hilly South Island has a smaller population than the North Island, from which it is separated by the 16-mi. (26-km) -wide Cook Strait. The South Island's largest city is Christchurch.

Kiwi capital

Kiwi fruit grow on vines. The brown, fuzzy skin covers emerald-green flesh dotted with edible black seeds. They were brought to New Zealand by Chinese missionaries at the beginning of the 1900s.

Maoris

The first settlers in New Zealand, the Maoris, arrived in sailing canoes from the Polynesian islands, to the north, in about A.D. 800. Captain Cook mapped the islands in 1769, and whalers, fur traders, and Christian missionaries began to settle on the coasts in the next century. Under the Treaty of Waitangi in 1840 the British persuaded Maori tribal chiefs to hand over their sovereignty in return for guarantees that protected ownership of their lands. But the British side of the bargain was quickly broken. New Zealand became a British colony, and settlers began pouring in.

By the end of the 1800s the Maoris had been decimated by warfare and disease. But their fortunes recovered, and now pure-blood Maoris and their descendants make up 14 percent of the population. In recent years new immigrants from South Pacific islands—notably from Samoa, Fiji, Tonga, and the Cook Islands—have settled in New Zealand.

The Maoris still preserve their traditional ways of life in some areas of the North Island such as the region of volcanic springs around

Cultural tradition

Maoris remember their roots by teaching children the history of the Maoris and about the particular group they belong to.

Rotorua, where houses are decorated with fine wooden carvings and statues of the protective gods sticking their tongues out in the traditional Maori greeting. The government has returned tribal lands to the Maoris, and Maori—now an official language of New Zealand—is taught in the country's schools.

Volcanic landscape

Rotorua is a volcanic region on the North Island. It is covered in steaming craters, boiling mud pools, and geysers spouting hot steam.

All Blacks

The *haka* (the Maori warrior dance) is performed by New Zealand's national rugby union team, the All Blacks (so-called because they wear a black uniform). They are one of the world's greatest rugby teams, producing international stars such as Jonah Lomu.

New Zealanders are also enthusiastic cricketers and yachtsmen, and they have excellent skiing facilities. Lawn bowling is a popular pastime, especially among older people. The open spaces at the center of many towns are often squared off with neatly mown bowling greens.

Rugby giant
All Blacks' star Jonah Lomu is one of the most famous rugby players in the world and a national hero in New Zealand.

New links

Many aspects of New Zealand life reflect its connections to Great Britain, and the British monarch is the head of state. In recent years there has been a decline in trade with Great Britain, and New Zealand has had to look elsewhere for export markets. It has developed closer trade links with other nations in the Pacific region and Asia.

New Zealand is a key member of the Pacific Islands Forum and has supported the drive to make the region nuclear-free. New Zealand does not have nuclear power. Instead electricity is generated mainly by hydroelectric power.

PACIFIC ISLANDS

Idyllic islands

French Polynesia attracts many visitors with its stylish vacation resorts and beautiful lagoons teeming with tropical fish.

Dotted across the vast, blue Pacific Ocean are some 25,000 islands, many of them tiny. The nations of the region are mostly made up of island groups scattered across the sea. Tonga, for example, consists of two large islands and about 150 smaller ones. The islands include some of the world's smallest nations—Nauru is just eight sq. mi. (20 sq km).

Excluding New Zealand, there are 12 independent countries in the region, but some island groups remain dependent on other larger countries. For example, the large island of New Caledonia is a French territory, as is French Polynesia, which includes Tahiti. Hawaii is a U.S. state, and Guam and American Samoa (not to be confused with neighboring Samoa, which is independent) are U.S. territories. Northern Mariana is also closely associated with the U.S. The tiny island of Pitcairn is a British territory, and Easter Island belongs to Chile, a South American country.

Three groups

In the 1800s the islands of the South Pacific were divided by geographers into three groups— Melanesia, Polynesia, and Micronesia. Melanesia consists of the larger islands in the southwest of the region—Papua New Guinea, the Solomon Islands, Vanuatu, and Fiji. They are inhabited by people whose ancestors traveled to the islands from Southeast Asia about 40,000 years ago. They developed a way of life based on growing yams and raising pigs— still the basis of farming there today.

Over time new waves of people headed farther east in search of new islands to settle. They traveled in large sailing canoes to the islands now called Polynesia, which include Hawaii, Easter Island, Tuvalu, Samoa, and Tonga. The Polynesians had their own language, gods, and ways of life, creating a distinctive and connected culture—all the more remarkable because it covered such a huge area.

The Polynesians were impressive navigators. They used their knowledge of the wind, stars, and flight patterns of seabirds to find their way from island to island across vast areas of open sea. Many islanders still have these skills and use them to move around the ocean, often in wooden outrigger sailing canoes, whose design has changed little for hundreds of years.

The third group is Micronesia, a peppering of small islands or island groups that spreads most of the way across the central belt of the Pacific. Palau, the Federated States of Micronesia, the Marshall Islands, Nauru, and Kiribati make up Micronesia.

Island dancer

Dancing is an important cultural tradition to the people of Micronesia. Men and women dance in separate groups, and the dancing is often accompanied by unison chanting.

Foreign influences

European explorers and traders first visited the Pacific Islands over 300 years ago. Christian missionaries came to the region from the late 1700s, and most islands are now Christian. During the 1800s Great Britain, France, Germany, and the U.S. took over many of the islands as colonies. They developed huge plantations, growing crops such as sugarcane and pineapples.

The British created huge sugarcane plantations in Fiji and brought in people from India to work on them. Now nearly half the population of Fiji is Asian.

Nauru, once a British colony, had rich deposits of phosphate— seabird dung— which was extracted and sold as fertilizer.

Worship

More than half of the people of Fiji are Christian. Music and singing form a large part of worship in the country's churches.

Most of this has now gone, but Nauru still lives off the profits, which were carefully invested abroad, notably in property in Australia.

Since winning their independence in the 1900s the islands have been looking for ways to support their economies in the long term. Most of them have only limited natural resources, and plantation crops do not provide big profits. One new major source of income is fishing. Countries such as the U.S., Japan, Korea, and Taiwan pay large sums of money to many of the Pacific nations for permission to fish in their waters.

Cyclones and volcanoes

The Pacific Islands straddle the equator, and they have a hot, humid climate. The more mountainous islands receive plenty of rain, which drops when the moisture-laden clouds rise up the hills and cool down.

Every year the heat over the ocean stirs the air into a spiraling funnel of very strong winds called cyclones. They move across the region, ripping up everything in their path.

Another danger comes from deep beneath earth. The Pacific Islands cover a very unstable part of earth's crust, where tectonic

Stormy lands

The Pacific Islanders often have to cope with cyclones ripping apart their towns and villages.

plates are slowly colliding. This pushes up volcanoes and causes earthquakes and tsunamis (fast, destructive waves).

In fact many Pacific Islands are volcanic in origin. They were formed when the tops of volcanoes pushed up from the seabed.

However, volcanoes, earthquakes, and tsunamis can cause destruction, sometimes wiping out entire villages, killing many, and leaving survivors without food or homes.

Natural riches

Volcanoes create very rich soil. This, combined with plenty of warmth and rain, means that plants generally grow very well in the Pacific region. Many of the islanders grow their own fruit and vegetables in gardens next to their villages. They produce yams, papayas, coconuts, and pumpkins. Fishermen make good catches in the still, shallow lagoons created by coral reefs or in the deep sea beyond the reefs, bringing in perch, shark, and tuna.

Coconut palms provide wood and leaves to make simple thatched houses. Villages in Samoa, for example, consist of very simple, open-sided dwellings, like roofed platforms, raised above the ground on stones. This design works well in the hot and humid climate. Walls of matting are used only to keep out troublesome breezes. There is very little furniture, and people sleep on mats. Villages are closely knit and sociable, usually formed around families and clans, and run by village headmen and a council of elders.

Ocean wonderland
The seas of the Pacific Ocean are home to beautiful coral reefs and abundant and varied sea life, including tropical fish and sponges.

On the smaller islands the sea is never far away. On the larger islands there are high volcanic hills, tropical forests and remote plains and river valleys. In some Melanesian islands there are natives living far inland who have had very little contact with the outside world. Over the centuries these isolated villages developed their own languages, with the result that Papua New Guinea has more than 800 languages and the Solomons have over 70. Many people in this region also speak pidgin, a shared language used for trading.

Heavy load
Villagers in Papua New Guinea carry firewood in bilum bags strapped to their heads. The bags are made from sago palm leaves.

Ancient and modern

The long-isolated communities of Melanesia still preserve many aspects of their individual cultures. In northern Papua New Guinea, for example, the people of the Sepik River area produce sacred carvings of their ancestor spirits and make masks to use in ritual dances. Many villages have elaborately carved cult-centers or "spirit houses," where only men are allowed. In the highlands clans wearing body paint gather for festivals of music and dance, wearing extravagant outfits made of grasses, shells, beads, and feathers. But these days the adornments may also be made of crushed tin cans, and some participants arrive by jeep.

Each year, as part of a festival after the yam harvest in the Pentecost Islands of Vanuatu, young men throw themselves off 82-ft. (25-m) -high wooden towers with their ankles attached to long vines—the original bungee jumping.

One unusual effect of long isolation was the development of "cargo cults" in Melanesia, particularly in Vanuatu. Whole religions, mixing local myths and Christianity, developed around foreign messiah figures who magically brought rich cargoes of goods by ship or plane.

The capital cities of many of the Pacific Island nations are modern. They have airports, satellite links, bus services, air-conditioned buildings, and international banks. But the islanders still follow many traditions. For example, the men and women of Tonga still wear stiff *ta'ovala* skirts made of woven pandanus palm mats. The people of Tonga, Fiji, and Samoa wear feltlike tapa cloth made from the pounded bark of mulberry trees and painted with patterns. The mildly narcotic drink kava, prepared from the root of a pepper plant, is still drunk with informal ceremony in Vanuatu, Fiji, Samoa, and Tonga and some islands of Micronesia.

Hopes for tourism

Most of the islands are very small, and many people leave to make new lives for themselves in New Zealand, Australia, or the U.S. There are

Beauty contest
As part of one Papua New Guinea festival women take part in a beauty contest. Not only judged on their beauty, they are also judged on skills in body painting and dancing.

80,000 Pacific Islanders in Australia alone.

Meanwhile more visitors are coming to the region—but this time on vacation. The Pacific Islands represent a tourist dream of white-sand beaches, blue seas, warm sun, and idyllic cottages beneath the coconut palms. Fiji, in particular, is developing its tourist facilities and now welcomes about 350,000 visitors each year. Tourists come to stay in the large resorts but also to hike in the tropical forests, climb volcanoes, dive among the coral reefs, and sail to remote islands.

Tourism brings valuable foreign income to the islands, and the nations of the Pacific Islands want to use tourism as a means of promoting and strengthening their own culture. Tourism gives them a reason to preserve their traditions of dance and music, cooking, basket weaving, and wood carving.

Tourism hopes
Many of the Pacific Island nations see tourism as an important source of income and are developing their tourist facilties.

 **AUSTRALIA**

Capital
Canberra
Area
2,937,800 sq. mi.
Population
19,357,594
Population density
7 per sq. mi.
Life expectancy
77 (m); 83 (f)
Religion
Christianity
Languages
English plus about 200 aboriginal languages
Adult literacy rate
100 percent
Currency
Australian dollar

 **FEDERATED STATES OF MICRONESIA**

Capital
Palikir
Area
271 sq. mi.
Population
134,597
Population density
497 per sq. mi.
Life expectancy
67 (m); 71 (f)
Religion
Christianity
Languages
English, Trukese, Pohnpeian, Yapese
Adult literacy rate
90 percent
Currency
U.S. dollar

 FIJI

Capital
Suva
Area
7,000 sq. mi.
Population
844,330
Population density
120 per sq. mi.
Life expectancy
66 (m); 71 (f)
Religions
Christianity, Hinduism, Islam
Languages
Fijian, Hindustani, English
Adult literacy rate
91 percent
Currency
Fijian dollar

Rocky land

Australia is home to some striking landscapes. These strange rock formations are in the Pinnacles Desert in Western Australia.

KIRIBATI

Capital
Bairiki
Area
277 sq. mi.
Population
94,149
Population density
340 per sq. mi.
Life expectancy
57 (m); 63 (f)
Religion
Christianity
Languages
Gilbertese, English
Adult literacy rate
90 percent
Currency
Australian dollar

 **MARSHALL ISLANDS**

Capital
Majuro
Area
70 sq. mi.
Population
70,822
Population density
1,012 per sq. mi.
Life expectancy
64 (m); 68 (f)
Religion
Christianity
Languages
English, Marshallese, Japanese
Adult literacy rate
91 percent
Currency
U.S. dollar

 NAURU

Capital
No official capital
Area
8 sq. mi.
Population
12,088
Population density
1,511 per sq. mi.
Life expectancy
58 (m); 65 (f)
Religion
Christianity
Languages
Nauruan, English
Adult literacy rate
99 percent
Currency
Australian dollar

 NEW ZEALAND

Capital
Wellington
Area
103,600 sq. mi.
Population
3,864,129
Population density
37 per sq. mi.
Life expectancy
75 (m); 81 (f)
Religion
Christianity
Languages
English, Maori
Adult literacy rate
100 percent
Currency
New Zealand dollar

 PALAU

Capital
Koror
Area
177 sq. mi.
Population
19,092
Population density
108 per sq. mi.
Life expectancy
66 (m); 72 (f)
Religions
Christianity, Modekngei
Languages
Palauan, English , Sonsorolese, Angaur, Japanese, Tobi
Adult literacy rate
98 percent
Currency
U.S. dollar

PAPUA NEW GUINEA

Capital
Port Moresby
Area
174,200 sq. mi.
Population
5,049,055
Population density
29 per sq. mi.
Life expectancy
61 (m); 66 (f)
Religions
Christianity, traditional beliefs
Languages
English, Motu, and many local languages
Adult literacy rate
72 percent
Currency
Kina

SAMOA

Capital
Apia
Area
1,100 sq. mi.
Population
179,058
Population density
163 per sq. mi.
Life expectancy
67 (m); 72 (f)
Religion
Christianity
Languages
Samoan, English
Adult literacy rate
100 percent
Currency
Tala

 **SOLOMON ISLANDS**

Capital
Honiara
Area
10,600 sq. mi.
Population
480,442
Population density
45 per sq. mi.
Life expectancy
69 (m); 74 (f)
Religion
Christianity
Languages
English, Melanesian, and
other Polynesian languages
Adult literacy rate
54 percent
Currency
Solomon Islands dollar

 TONGA

Capital
Nuku'alofa
Area
289 sq. mi.
Population
104,227
Population density
361 per sq. mi.
Life expectancy
66 (m); 71 (f)
Religion
Christianity
Languages
Tongan, English
Adult literacy rate
93 percent
Currency
Pa'anga

 TUVALU

Capital
Funafuti Atoll
Area
10 sq. mi.
Population
10,991
Population density
1,099 per sq. mi.
Life expectancy
65 (m); 69 (f)
Religion
Christianity
Languages
Tuvaluan, English
Adult literacy rate
95 percent
Currency
Australian dollar

 VANUATU

Capital
Port-Vila
Area
5,700 sq. mi.
Population
192,910
Population density
34 per sq. mi.
Life expectancy
60 (m); 62 (f)
Religions
Christianity, traditional beliefs
Languages
Bislama, English, French
Adult literacy rate
36 percent
Currency
Vatu

INDEX

ACKNOWLEDGMENTS

1 Robert Harding. 2-3 Still Pictures/Neil Cooper. 4-5 Still Pictures/Harmut Schwarzbach. 6-7 Anderson Geographics. 8-9 Robert Harding. 10 Trip/A. Tovy: T; Robert Harding/Gavin Hellier: B. 11 Hutchison Library/John Wright. 12 Robert Harding/Wally Herbert. 13 Anderson Geographics. 14-15 Still Pictures/Michael Sewell. 15 Still Pictures/Brian & Cherry Alexander. 16 Robert Harding/F. Jackson. 17 Robert Harding/Rover PH/Explorer. 18-19 Anderson Geographics. 20-21 Robert Harding/Gavin Hellier. 21 Hutchison Library/Andrew Sole. 22 Hutchison Library/Billie Rafaeli. 22-23 Still Pictures/Brian & Cherry Alexander. 24 Trip/V. Kolpakov. 24-25 Trip/J. Greenberg. 26-27 Robert Harding/Roy Rainford. 27 John Meek. 28 Robert Harding/Adam Woolfitt: T; Hutchison Library/Nancy Durrell McKenna: B. 29 Collections/Graeme Peacock. 30-31 Still Pictures/Ron Giling. 31 Trip/B. Turner. 32 Hutchison Library: L; Trip: R. 33 Still Pictures/Thomas Raupach. 34-35 Rex Features/Sipa Press. 35 Trip/A. Tovy. 36-37 Still Pictures/Thomas Raupach. 37 Still Pictures/Wim Van Cappellen. 38 Hutchison Library: T; Trip/C. Gibson: B. 39 Trip/J.D. Dallet. 40-41 View Pictures/Dennis Gilbert. 41 Hutchison Library/Edward Parker. 42-43 Still Pictures/Pierre Gleizes. 43 Still Pictures/Mark Edwards. 44 Corbis/Owen Franklin, T; Corbis/Vittoriano Rastelli, B. 45 Still Pictures/Calvert/UNEP. 46-47 Hutchison Library/J.G. Fuller. 47 Hutchison Library/Liba Taylor. 48-49 Hutchison Library/T.E. Clark. 49 Hutchison Library. 50 Hutchison Library/Nigel Howard. 51 Hutchison Library/Nick Haslam. 52-53 Robert Harding/C. Bowman. 54-55 Hutchison Library/Liba Taylor. 55 Hutchison Library/Vadim Kvorinin: T; Hutchison Library/Andrey Zvoznikov: B. 56-57 Hutchison Library/Andrey Zvoznikov. 60 Hutchison Library/Robert Francis. 61 Hutchison Library/Nigel Howard. 63 Hutchison Library/John Egan. 65 Hutchison Library/Nancy Durrell McKenna. 66 Still Pictures/David Drain. 67 DRK/A. Kaye. 68 Anderson Geographics. 69 Robert Harding/I. Vanderharst. 70 Trip/Viesti Collection. 70-71 Hutchison Library. 72-73 Robert Harding. 74 Trip/Viesti Collection. 74-75 Trip/S. Grant. 75 Still Pictures/Peter Arnold Inc./Jeff Greenberg. 76 Still Pictures/Thomas Laird. 76-77 Robert Harding/Paul Van Riel. 77 Robert Harding. 78 Still Pictures/Julio Etchart. 78-79 DRK/Mark Gibson. 79 DRK/David Woodfall. 80 Trip/T. Freeman: T; Allsport/Clive Brunskill: B. 80-81 Allsport/Paul Severn. 82 Rex Features/Mike Segar. 82-83 Rex Features/Gary Calton. 84-85 DRK/Darrell Gulin. 85 Still Pictures/Jim Wark: T; NASA: B. 86 Popperfoto. 86-87 Rex Features/Alastair Pullen. 88 Robert Harding. 89 Rex Features/Sipa Press/Gustavo Ferrari. 90-91 Robert Harding: L; Hutchison Library/Nancy Durrell McKenna: R. 92 Robert Harding/J.C. Teyssier. 93 Hutchison Library/Brian Moser. 94 Trip/M. Shirley. 94-95 Robert Harding. 96 Still Pictures/John Cancalosi. 97 Hutchison Library/Juliet Highet: T; Hutchison Library/Edward Parker: B. 98 Still Pictures/Mark Edwards. 98-99 Hutchison Library/Robert Francis. 100-101 Hutchison Library/Philip Wolmuth. 101 Hutchison Library/Jeremy Horner. 102 Still Pictures/Paul Harrison. 102-103 Hutchison Library/John Hatt. 104-105 Hutchison Library/Robert Francis. 106-107 Still Pictures/Nigel Harrison. 107 Still Pictures/Jorgen Schytte. 108 Hutchison Library/Robert Francis. 112 Rex Features/Stewart Cook. 113 Still Pictures/Chris Martin. 114 Anderson Geographics. 115 Still Pictures/Ron Giling. 116-117 Still Pictures/Josh Schachter. 117 Hutchison/Jeremy Horner. 118 Hutchison Library/Robert Francis. 118-119 Hutchison Library/Eric Lawrie. 119 Still Pictures/Ron Giling. 120-121 Hutchison Library/Robert Francis. 121 Hutchison Library/Jeremy Horner. 122 Still Pictures/John Maier. 122-123 Hutchison Library/Jeremy Horner. 123 Hutchison Library/Richard House. 124 Still Pictures/John Maier. 124-125 Hutchison Library. 127 Still Pictures/Nigel Dickinson. 129 Still Pictures/Muriel Nicolotti. 130 Anderson Geographics. 131-133 Hutchison Library/Michael Macintyre. 133 Corbis/Paul Souders. 134-135 Still Pictures/John Isaacs: T; Robert Harding: B. 135 AFP/Corbis. 136 Corbis. 136-137 Corbis/Buddy Mays. 138 David Monfarrige. 138-139 Hutchison Library. 139 Popperfoto/Reuters. 140-141 Robert Harding. 141 Still Pictures/Demi-Unep. 142 Still Pictures/Ron Giling. 142-143 Hutchison Library. 143 Ron Giling/Still Pictures. 144 Robert Harding. 145 Still Pictures/Margaret Wilson. 146-147 Hutchison Library. 147 Popperfoto. 148 Steve McDonagh. 149 Hutchison Library: T; Corbis/David & Peter Turnley: B. 150 Still Pictures/Roger de la Harpe. 150-151 National Geographic Image Collection/Chris Johns. 161 Still Pictures/Ron Giling. 162-163 Anderson Geographics. 164-165 Corbis/K.M. Westermann. 166 Hutchison Library/Nigel Howard. 166-167 Roy Williams. 167 Corbis/Reuters/New Media Inc. 168-169 Still Pictures/Adrian Arbib. 169 Popperfoto/Duncan Willetts: T; Still Pictures/Bojan Brecel: B. 170-171 Robert Harding/Tom Ang. 172-173 Robert Harding/David Beatty. 173 Still Pictures/Gil Moti. 174 Still Pictures/Mark Edwards. 174-176 Michael Freeman. 177 Corbis/Popperfoto/Reuters. 178 Robert Harding. 179 Corbis/Jonathan Blair. 180-181 Still Pictures/John Isaacs. 182-183 Michael Freeman. 184 Still Pictures/Ron Giling: T; Still Pictures/Shehzad Nooran: B. 184-185 Popperfoto/Reuters/Pawel Kopcynski. 186 Robert Harding/James Strachan. 186-187 Still Pictures/Jean-Leo Dugas. 187 Still Pictures/Andy Crump. 193 Robert Harding/Explorer. 194-195 Still Pictures/Adrian Arbib. 196 Still Pictures/Ingrid Moorjohn. 196-197 Hutchison Library/Robert Francis. 198-199 Still Pictures/Julio Etchart. 199 Hutchison Library/Jeremy Horner. 200 Richard & Sally Greenhill. 201 Still Pictures. 202-203 Hutchison Library/Maurice Harvey. 203 Hutchison Library/Robert Francis. 204 Robert Harding. 204-205 Hutchison Library/Jon Burbank. 206 Hutchison Library/Jeremy Horner. 206-207 Hutchison Library/Trevor Page. 208-209 Still Pictures/Jorgen Schytte. 209 Karen Aniola. 210 Still Pictures/Joerg Boethling. 211 Still Pictures/UNEP. 212-213 Karen Aniola. 213 Hutchison Library. 214-215 Still Pictures/Jorgen Scytte. 215 Still Pictures/Tim Page. 216-217 Hutchison Library/William Holtby. 218 Hutchison Library/P. Collomb. 219 Karen Aniola. 220-221 Robert Harding/N. Wheeler. 222 Still Pictures/Tim Page. 223 Still Pictures/Roland Seitre. 224-225 Anderson Geographics. 226-227 Hutchison Library/Ian Lloyd. 227 Still Pictures/Roland Seitre. 228-229 Still Pictures/John Cancalosi. 229 Hutchison Library. 230 Corbis/Robert Garvey. 230-231 Still Pictures/Roland Seitre. 232-233 Hutchison Library/Robert Francis. 234-235 Hutchison Library/Nick Haslam. 235 Trip/Ask Images. 236 Trip/Graham Pritchard. 236-237 Still Pictures/Vincent Bretagnolle. 237 Popperfoto. 238-239 Still Pictures/Yves Lefevre. 239 Still Pictures/Reportage/Carlos Guarita. 240 Hutchison Library/Mary Jelliffe. 240-241 Still Pictures/Gerard & Margi Moss. 242-243 Still Pictures/Fred Bavendam. 243 Still Pictures/Andy Crump. 244 Still Pictures/Richard West. 244-245 Hutchison Library/Bernard Regent. 246 Still Pictures/Dani/Jeske.

T = Top   L = Left
B = Bottom   R = Right